Flowers For Cina

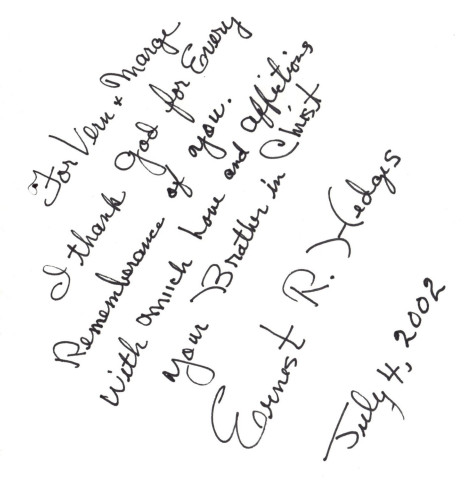

For Vern + Marge

I thank God for Every
Remembrance of you.

with much love and afflictions

your Brother in Christ

Earnest R. Hedges

July 4, 2002

Flowers For Cina

**Romance in Florence, Italy
Life Story Of Ernest R. Hedges**

Flowers For Cina

ERNEST R. HEDGES

ILLUSTRATED BY JANE C. MEIER
With an Afterword by Dorothy (Dotti) Olsen and Jane Meier

Writers Club Press
San Jose New York Lincoln Shanghai

Flowers For Cina

Writers Club Press
an imprint of iUniverse, Inc.

For information address:
iUniverse, Inc.
5220 S. 16th St., Suite 200
Lincoln, NE 68512
www.iuniverse.com

ISBN: 0-595-22737-6

Printed in the United States of America

Dedicated
To My Four Wonderful Children

Trees For Dorothy
Branches For Jonathan
Roots For David
Leaves For Jane

Epigraph

Roots For David

I decided to write my story because my son David asked about my family tree. When children are growing up they are not interested in family history. If I should bring the subject up the answer would usually be, "I know Dad, when you were young you milked ten cows before breakfast and walked to school." It wasn't that they didn't care, they were not interested. However, when they married and had children of their own they wanted to know more of the family history so they could pass it on to their children.

And so it was with David. One time he asked, "Dad, I don't know anything about your family history, fill me in." Now he was interested. That started me to thinking. I didn't know much about my family tree. I didn't know where my mother was born or anything about her childhood. The same could be said about my father. I would give anything to know more about my parent's background and everyday life when they were growing up, guess I never asked! It occurred to me if I started writing a few facts about myself, in two or three generations future grandchildren would know.

David asked, but I am writing to all of my children: Dorothy Jean, Jane Carol, David Ernest, and Jonathan Craig, also to my grandchildren and to their children.

People who have read my story have said it has given them the idea to do the same for their children. One of the many reasons for writing "Flowers For Cina," is to encourage parents to write about their everyday life. There comes a time in life we want to know more about our heritage. I have enjoyed writing this immensely and recommend everyone do the same.

List of Illustrations

Foreword

By David Ernest Hedges

It was the worst of times; it was the best of times.

While Europe was held riveted to the rhythm of jackboots goose-stepping on ancient cobblestone, a thin callow youth somewhere in Kansas was preparing to embark on the journey of his life. He was preparing to go to war and to his fate. Who can know what his fate will be——In uncertain times, such as these, it could mean death, capture or defeat. It could also mean triumph, glory or victory. Certainly on the eve of his departure it meant a journey unlike any he had ever known. It had to be a time of fear and trepidation, but also one of excitement and anticipation.

It is odd to think how the little things in life can sometimes influence out comes of a lifetime. "A left turn instead of a right" "arriving five minutes early," these things can sometimes mean the difference between life and death, fame and fortune, or misery and happiness.

Other times there are great cataclysmic events that transform the world forever after. Strange to think that a demonic form such as Adolph Hitler could have had such a transforming effect on all western civilization, as we know it.

Without Hitler and the ensuing world conflict there is no rapid ascent of America, no overnight technological explosion. There is no rise to prominence of Winston Churchill, no Eisenhower, and no Ernie and Cina, at least not together.

In the ultimate triumph of good over evil, millions of baby boomers from mixed ancestry; English American/Italian-American forged together to create a new America. Yes, this was truly a time of history in titanic proportion:

It was the time of Eisenhower, McArthur, Churchill, Roosevelt, Stalin, and HEDGES.

Preface

Hedges History

Hedges is an English name. It has been told that one of our ancestors lived in London. He was accused of stealing rabbits and to avoid arrest escaped to America. A very noble beginning! Father said he would receive letters from London telling about a fortune that he should claim. He never did. I did know that my father lived in Illinois, studied to be a lawyer but became a farmer instead. One of his brothers was the superintendent of public schools in Chicago. His brother, Charley, lived in Seward, Nebraska (the only brother I knew). Uncle Charley had three daughters; Elsie Rolfsmeier, Ida, who never married, and Emma Matzke. My father had two sisters. Aunt Effi Foote was the only sister I knew, who lived in Tokepa, Kansas and was blind in one eye. My father's parents, Caleb and Mary Hedges, lived to be 98 years old and are buried in Courtland, Kansas.

My mother's father, Henry Creighton was born in New York City. His parents came to America from Ireland during the potato famine in 1845. Grandma Creighton was also born in New York and her maiden name was Lyon. Mother had two brothers and one sister. Uncle Irvy and Uncle Art were married but had no children. Aunt Emma Findley had 5 children; Maynard, Kenneth, Pauline, Leland, and Eldon. Leland was killed in an airplane crash over the Gulf of Mexico during World War II. Aunt Emma at one time had a very large goiter, but it was successfully removed by surgery. Mother was a twin; her twin sister died at birth.

Grandpa Creighton lived to be 101 and 6 months and Grandma Creighton lived to be 95. They are buried in Seward, Nebraska.

I came from a family of 10 children, the following according to age: Pearl, Grace, Wilbur, Stella, Elmer, Hazel, Louise, and Lewis (twins), Ernest, and Eunice. My Grandpa Creighton had some Scottish blood in him so that makes me English and Scotch-Irish.

Acknowledgements

I would like to thank the following for their support and assistance on this book.

My son David who inspired me to write" Roots For David". My daughter Jane for spending endless hours arranging pictures and editing the manuscript for publication. My daughter Dorothy's suggestions and encouragement and my son Jonathan for spurring me on.

Lisa Meier, wife of my grandson David, for suggesting additional subtitles for my original book, Roots for David: Flowers For Cina, Trees For Dorothy, Branches for Jonathan, and Leaves for Jane. I choose to use Flowers For Cina with the others in dedication to my children.

The crew of proofreaders, Mary Schmaltz, Dorothy Olsen, Shannon Hayes, Patti Arteaga, Vivian Ferguson and Pastor Doug Hadley.

My teacher, Sandy Fox, who opened my eyes to the thrill of writing. "Show me don't tell". I consider myself an average student but since I am 90 years old I received an "A" for effort.

My oldest sister Pearl was an ardent reader and said, "Flowers For Cina" is a story everybody would enjoy. Pearl will celebrate her 107th birthday July 2002.

To my 10 grandchildren for their inspiration and encouragement and who added many pages to this book.

Thankfulness to the Grace of God, the agape love that makes it all worthwhile." Love others as God loved us and to forgive as Christ has forgiven us."

Introduction

Life Story Of Ernest R. Hedges

By

Ernest R. Hedges

I have no thrilling, hair raising war stories to tell my grandchildren; no scars or awards. (I received three Stars for serving in North Africa, Sicily, and Italy). There are many heroic stories that can be told, how one soldier laid down his life to save his platoon or a buddy. I carried no gun, but was within the sound of guns. An Evacuation Hospital, which I was part of, received the injured first, treated them and then transported them to a general hospital for further treatment.—-No, I was in no way a hero, but—-some times, things happen when we least expect it—**like falling in love** —-that is the thrilling story I can tell my grandkids!!

Chapter 1

The Kansas Years

It happened Halloween night, October 31, 1916. John Brown Country School always hosted a Halloween costume party, an event my mother would never miss. Tonight was no exception. John Brown, one-room, red country schoolhouse was located two miles west of Courtland, Kansas, and one mile west of the farm where I took my first breath, October 19, 1911. Our home was a ranch type house, unusual because two to three story homes were in style.

We were a large family, ten children all born at home and I was next to the youngest. So many children helped to keep my mother young. She loved to play games with us, like "handy, handy over" and "run sheep run." She really enjoyed dressing up for Halloween.

Halloween was my favorite fun night, and a harvest moon added to the suspense of the season. Unfortunately I was sick in bed and by evening my temperature started to climb. I couldn't go to the party and my oldest sister, Pearl, volunteered to stay home with me. How could my mother miss the party after she spent so much time making her costume? Very reluctantly, Mother went but she could always sense when something was wrong. She came home early to find my temperature 105 and my face yellow as a pumpkin.

Mother called Doctor Snyder. He recognized the symptoms and lost no time getting me in his Model T Ford and to the nearest hospital. Mother held me in her strong arms as the doctor explained I was in a crucial condition: my appendix had ruptured. What a treat and a thrill to ride in a car! We only had a buggy. I shall always remember that night ride. The full moon caused shifting shadows in the trees, and I am sure I saw buffaloes, and Indians at every curve in the road. When we arrived at the hospital and entered the door, the hot smelly air made me sick to my stomach. The last thing I remember the doctor saying was, "We have to operate immediately." I thought of the large butcher knife my mother used for cutting meat. They are going to cut me open!

In 1916 doctors in western Kansas didn't know much about appendicitis. Evidently they did something right because I pulled through. I still have a scar on my right side 6 inches long. I slowly recovered but the doctor said I shouldn't run and I should wear suspenders until my side healed. How humiliating! Only old men wore suspenders.

The day I left the hospital I saw a bright colored fire engine drawn by six horses. I never knew it was a fire engine until my mother told me. Courtland is so small it didn't even have a fire department.

Boys have a way of growing up and I was no exception. Being in a large family, we always found things to do. Dad insisted we do our chores and school work first, and then and only then, could we play. Our out door games were running games like "hide and seek" and baseball. We made the bats out of trunks of skinny trees. Indoors we played checkers or dominoes and a card game called, "pit." For my 12th birthday my brother Lewis (I called him Bob) gave me a bow and arrow he had made. We all took turns shooting it and to my surprise, as well as to the others, I hit the Bull's eye.

Two days before my 12th birthday something happened half way around the world that would change my life forever. On a very narrow street, made only for bicycles and carts in the heart of the most beautiful city, Florence, Italy, a midwife was frantically trying to find apartment 32.

(It was hard to tell where the street stopped and the buildings began. All were made of the same brick and stone.)

The midwife lost no time climbing the stairs to the 3rd floor, where a dim light marked the door number 32. A very gentle but excited man waited for the Midwife.

"What can I do?" He was talking more to himself than to the midwife.

The midwife replied, "I need lots of hot water and towels."

Just as the sun came up you could hear a wee little cry and the midwife announced, "It's a girl!"

She was named Teresa after her grandmother, the girl I would marry in 21 years. Her nickname was "CINA".

With no thought of tomorrow, I continued to play with my bow and arrow.

Chapter 2

Farming in Minnesota

Farming in Kansas, my father used to say, was a gamble, one good crop in seven years. Many times my Dad would cut Canadian thistles just to keep the cows alive through the winter. The soil in Kansas contains rich minerals, but was scarce in waterfall. This wasn't much of an incentive to farm in Kansas. When my oldest sister and her husband (Pearl and Claude Bettis) married, they moved to a hundred twenty acre farm near Oak Park, Minnesota, sixty miles north of Minneapolis.

In less than two years when I was 8, our family left the farm in Kansas and moved to a small town called Chasebrook in central Minnesota. I could never find it on the map. We arrived in mid-winter and from the train depot to the farm we rode in a bobsled. Heated bricks kept our feet warm. An old log cabin on the farm caused a lot of curiosity. It was well preserved, a relic from the past. We could see how the early settlers built their homes from trees and bonded them together with mud and clay. My Dad used it for a machine shed and a few stray cats made it their home. We soon moved to a larger farm near Milaca.

In Milaca I saw my first outside silent movie, "Charlie Chaplin". My brother Bob, and I would make kites and sometimes our string would be two miles long. We waxed the string to make it stronger. There were many things I remember about Milaca. Many times I would walk to town just to see the trains and listen for the whistle. I loved those huge engines with steam coming out of their nostrils.

The woods around our farm were covered with strange wild flowers. I remember one cold snowy Christmas in 1922 when my sister Grace and I dragged a Christmas tree home over the ice and snow. We decorated the tree with strings of popcorn and cranberries. Instead of candles we tied red crab apples to the branches. Christmas Eve we gathered around the tree, opened presents, and sang Christmas Carols.

We had an old piano in the living room and I would go in to figure out how to play the ivory keys. The first hymn I learned, with the help of my Mother, was "Pass me not, Gentle Savior." My Mother believed in God and even talked to Him. I knew my mother was somebody special.

My sister, Stella, became part of some startling history at Milaca high school.She organized the first girl's basketball team in Kansas. You never heard of girls playing basketball in 1920. Milaca and some other small towns formed a basketball league. Milaca High school had facilities for basketball but in other towns they played on dance floors. A national movement tried to keep girls out of sports. The girls wore bloomers and some considered it exploitation to wear bloomers in front of men. The girl's basketball league disbanded in 1922. Many years went by before they were allowed to play.

Milaca was a neat little town but did not offer the opportunities for work as Minneapolis did, 60 miles away. After finishing high school, my brothers and sisters flocked to the big city to find jobs.

To keep the family together my dad sold the farm, had an auction sale, pulled up our roots, and transplanted them to Minneapolis when I was 11 years old.

Chapter 3

Beautiful Minneapolis

Minneapolis has many beautiful lakes. I remember one Sunday afternoon my dad (we always called him Papa) took us to the shores of Lake Calahoon to hear President Coolridge speak. I felt very proud to see the President of the United States. The parks are especially beautiful, filled with lilac bushes, dahlias, thousands of gorgeous peonies, and roses. Minneapolis has twenty-two natural lakes within the city limits. On holidays and birthdays the family would gather together for a big home cooked meal and we spent the rest of the day playing "Rook," a popular bidding card game. The cards are number from 1 to 14, in 4 suits of 4 colors, black, green, red, and yellow. We would have 3 tables with 4 players at each table with partners. The winners worked their way to the head table.

A country boy at heart, it took me a long time to get used to the big city. We moved to Minneapolis in the spring. The snow melted and streets were filled with soupy-snow mixed with coal dust. The streets were never cleared; black dirty coal was delivered to the homes by bobsleds drawn by horses. We had fun trying to hook a ride, the bobsleds had huge runners and we just jumped on.

In the wintertime I loved the fresh fallen snow on the blue spruce trees, especially on Park Avenue where the rich people lived.

In the summertime, the ice wagon attracted us. We tried to catch the flying ice, as the iceman chipped the ice to fit the different size iceboxes— before refrigerators were invented. I looked forward to the one horse bakery wagon. My mother would buy those delicious sticky pecan rolls. I had the duty to go to Dunwoody Baking School and buy bread for the family. The students were learning how to bake and I would get fives loaves at five cents per loaf every other day.

One time at a neighborhood theater the management announced that the first woman to reach the stage who had ten children would receive a bag of groceries. My mother ran so fast she missed a step and fell flat to the floor and broke her nose. She received the prize.

My mother became a great admirer of Charles Lindberg and followed his flight crossing the Atlantic with great excitement. I made a crystal radio set with earphones and used the bedsprings for an antenna. What a mistake, for she glued herself to that set for two days and we had to get our own meals!

She also admired Bryd's Expedition to the North Pole in 1928. When the movie came out she had to see it. She caught a severe cold and blamed it on the movie.

Once while walking down Hennipen Ave. I saw a parade and it turned out to be Al Smith, who was running for President against Hoover in 1928. I shall always remember the campaign speeches in 1932 by Herbert Hoover and Franklin D. Roosevelt. I was for Hoover. Hoover was

President in my last two years of high school and he said, "Prosperity was just around the corner." That was good enough for me.

I fell in and out of love couple times when going to grade school. One time I walked with a girl and carried her books. My friends teased me so much I didn't want to go back to school. The next morning I locked myself in the bathroom and threw the key out the window. Wouldn't you know, my mother had an extra key and told me to go to school and not to be late. This was about the time of the great depression, in 1929; soup lines were common. My dad would never go on relief. Being a hard worker, he always provided for the family. He insisted we all graduate from high school. My mother, being very frugal and parsimonious was able to keep food on the table. We had bean soup and Spanish rice often. The depression didn't affect us; we thought it was normal.

Walking home from school one day I heard people talking about an accident. A nurse had fallen asleep at the wheel, lost control of her car and hit a man. I didn't know it was my dad until I arrived home. He never regained consciousness and died a week later. A neighbor woman asked my mother to go to a séance with her. Mother very politely said, "No thanks, all I need is My Heavenly Father."

One year after my father's death my sister Stella discovered she had a small benign tumor that could be easily removed with minor surgery. My sister went to the hospital by herself. Since it was a minor operation the doctor decided to take her appendix out at the same time. The day after the surgery the doctor found out he had made a serious mistake that resulted in a second operation; her intestines were twisted. It proved to be fatal. She was the only one in the family that could sing and the Sunday she died she sang "Nearer My God To Thee," even though she was in great pain. She was 29.

During my high school years I spent my summer vacations at Pearl and Claude's farm near Milaca. I guess it was an escape from the big city. I loved to tend to the animals especially the horses. Training wild horses from Montana gave us lot of excitement. Wild horses were sold way below normal price. The first step in training wild horses is to get them used to the halter and the bridle. The next step is to convince the horses to let you ride them. This may take days. First you put a blanket over their backs, then your coat, and then you jump on and hang on for dear life! Once I was riding my favorite horse and got too close to the marsh (I called it the sinking forest). What a crazy idea but I wanted to explore it. The horse barely got out of the soggy ground. I jumped off the horse, but the horse went down and down just like in quicksand. It really scared me. After ten minutes the horse managed to get out and I washed the mud off and never told my brother-in-law. He had warned me never to even get close to the low lands.

I didn't like racking and putting up hay, too tedious. I had fun mowing hay because mowing around a field would scare the rabbits to the center and the last time around the rabbits would all jump out. In the fall I did the plowing. I enjoyed seeing the many black birds following the plow to catch a nice juicy worm as I turned over the good smelling earth.

On weekends some of the family would come to the farm and we had plenty of fresh fried chicken and Claude's famous homemade ice cream. We picked wild strawberries in the meadow. Were they ever good; small, but good! You have never tasted strawberries until you taste the wild ones. Hazelnuts were plentiful. Don, Vivian, and Mary-Lou were the only children when I went to the farm. Millie and Verna Mae were born after I went to Nebraska.

I graduated from Central High School in Minneapolis in January 1931. All of my brothers and sisters were married now except my youngest sister, Eunice. My mother broke up house- keeping and took Eunice and myself to live with our Grandparents, Henry and Mary Creighton, in Seward Nebraska.

(Top Row) Grace, Elmer, Pearl, Wilbur, Lewis, and Stella
(Bottom Row) Hazel, Elmer (Father) Ernest, Eunice, Lottie, (Mother) and Louise
1929

Chapter 4

Camping in the Ozarks

My mother's father fought in the Civil War and loved to tell how he disobeyed orders to see Abraham Lincoln. The command was to stand at attention. Grandpa turned his head to get a glimpse of the famous man. He fought at Gettysberg and in the Battle of Bull Run where his twin brother was killed at his side. My grandparents, Henry and Mary Creighton, traveled from New York State to Nebraska in a covered wagon pulled by oxen in 1870. He lived to be 101 years and 6 months. On his 100th birthday he climbed to the top of his house and nailed one shingle. My grandmother was great and loved to make soft molasses cookies. Around the house she always grew petunias and nasturtiums.

My oldest brother Wilbur, who lived in Minneapolis, moved back to the old farm place in Kansas in 1934. He moved from Minnesota to Kansas in a Ford touring car and a 4-wheel trailer with his wife, Ann, and their two children, Betty-Ann and Joyce. They stopped in Seward and my mother and I joined them the rest of the way to the farm. My mother stayed for a couple months before returning to Seward and I stayed on the farm with my brother.

When my poor sister-in-law first entered the house, she threw her apron over her head and cried. The house needed cleaning, and the walls were bare and we only had boxes for chairs. We had buckwheat pancakes three times a day. It was like pioneer days. The neighbors gave us an old fashion shower. Some brought chickens, pigs, one cow, and a calf. Some also brought corn for planting, garden seeds, and canned goods. The neighbors and friends were great. It wasn't long until the boxes were replaced with chairs and the menu included more than pancakes.

I enjoyed helping my brother and his family to be established on the farm. There were several young people my age and we had many good times, especially on Saturday nights. Everybody in those days went to town on Saturday night. We would enjoy a band concert and then take in a movie. The drug store had a soda fountain, which was a favorite hang out. We would fill up on malted milk, ice cream, and root beer.

After two years, things were going fine on the farm so I decided it was time for me to go on my own. The railroad tracks went across our farm leaving five acres on one side. My brother made a deal with me and said I could plant anything I wanted to in the five acres that I could sell.

It was already late in the summer, so I decided to plant corn. My brother thought it was a poor idea because he already had eighty acres of corn. As it turned out I had more corn on my five acres than he had on his eighty. The late summer rains came just at the right time. Needless to say I had no corn to sell as it all went to feed the animals, however, I had saved some money and I was anxious to hit the road. Later that fall a neighbor sold some beef cattle and was shipping them to Kansas City. He received two free passes to ride in the caboose and he gave one to me. The last car of a stock train is called a caboose.

I had answered an ad in a farm magazine and made a $5.00 deposit to buy a cabin on the James River in Galena, Missouri. My idea was to get rich by growing mushrooms in the Ozarks.

I knew it was time for me to be on my own, so leaving wasn't so bad. Before leaving Courtland I stopped in to see my Sunday-School teacher, Miss Olive Ritter. She wore funny hats but we all liked her. I told her of my plans. To my surprise she said, "Great, I'll pray for you." Just the encouragement I needed.

I rode to Kansas City in the caboose of a stock train. From there I took a bus to Springfield and then to Galena. Now to find my cabin! Galena is near the now famous city of Branson, Missouri.

My first encounter with hillbillies proved to be interesting and friendly. Finally, I found one that knew the location of my cabin and he offered to take me there. It turned out he was my nearest neighbor. To be neighborly, he invited me in to his shack for a cup of coffee. (Now at this time in my life I wasn't much of a coffee drinker.) His wife insisted she made the best coffee in these parts of the woods.

The reason, "I never "warsh" the coffee pot," she said. Her pot was always on the stove and she just added coffee and more water. How can you be grateful for the worst cup of coffee you ever tasted? I figured my stomach could handle it. "You are very kind," I told her.

Bare floors, nude walls, and undressed windows described my cabin, not exactly what the ad said. What can you expect for $5.00? However, it did have a roof and four walls. My new friend said the fellow before me stayed just two days.

I shall never forget my first night under the twinkling stars. The cabin had no bed, no stove, and the mercury began to fall. The chilly air made me shiver. There were plenty of old trees and branches so I made a nice fire with dry wood and lots of logs. The warmth of the fire comforted me. I spent the night under the light of the moon and before morning it started to snow.

When the sun rose the next morning, the beauty over-whelmed me as the frost and ice on the branches sparkled like diamonds. Only the Creator could paint such a scene. There were blue jays, cardinals, and birds I never saw before. What a peaceful sight! "My Grace is sufficient for you." The words of the Apostle Paul took on a new meaning. What more do we need? Christ, God's beloved Son became poor that we could became rich. It is the greatest expression of Love and Grace. My mother had instilled in me a love for the Bible.

I was still completely enthralled by the beauty of the morning, but suddenly I felt something moving at my feet. I think my heart missed a beat. To my surprise there was a small Fox Terrier curled up by my feet. We were the best of friends the rest of the summer.

The Ozark Mountains are beautiful and interesting. I was near "Shepherd of the Hill Country." There are many cold springs to cool off and caves to explore.

Times were tough. It was a very dry summer. I had a job picking tomatoes but they dried up, my money was gone and there was no food in the cabin. I had lived on wild mushrooms and berries until they dried up. I wondered if the Lord would send me food by a raven like He did to Elijah. I felt like the prodigal son, thinking of all the good food back home.

Suddenly there was a knock at the door. There stood a man, old enough to be my father, and in his hands he had a large plate of food. Roast beef, potatoes, gravy, green peas, bread, and even a piece of cake. He said they expected company that didn't come and wondered if I could use some food. Could I! I thanked him and he was gone. I never saw the man before and never saw him again. Elijah had nothing on me. God still has his ravens! Even my little dog had a big bone to chew on that night.

The next day a man who lived a short way from me came to see me. He had built a summerhouse in the Ozarks. It turned out he knew my grandfather because he was from Seward. The purpose of his visit was to offer me a job. I jumped at the chance; there was no other choice! When one has no food and no money the alternative is to work. He, who doesn't work, doesn't eat. A lesson I learned early in life.

Near my cabin, was a horseshoe bend in the James River. You could take a canoe for three days and return one half mile from where you started. It became an attraction for fishermen. After a time, living in the "Hills" became very boring and lonely. My wondering spirit soon told me it was time to move on.

The saddest words in the Bible I believe are found in Hebrews 3:19. God told Israel they could not enter into the Promised Land because of their unbelief. I believed God had something different for me. No longer did I believe the Ozarks to be the Promised Land. "God take me out of here!" I prayed.

Days went by, even weeks and nothing happened. I knew I didn't belong here but what could I do? The people I stayed with didn't have enough work for me so I just worked for my room and board.

One beautiful morning I received a letter from my sister Hazel. They were taking a trip and wanted to see the Ozarks, could they come and see me? (An answer to my prayer) My sister never forgave me for the terrible roads, just about ruined their tires. When I saw my sister, she was the most beautiful person in the world. I rode with my sister and her husband, Leonard, as far north as I could, then hitchhiked west to Seward, Nebraska, arriving at grandpa's house late in March 1935. By this time my mother had returned from the farm to be with her father.

Chapter 5

Grandfather Creighton

My grandfather was a Civil War hero but had some strange notions. The cannon that killed his twin brother made him stone deaf. Grandpa wouldn't let me have a radio. He thought the radio would attract lightning and cause a storm. Well, I guess I shouldn't blame him. This same house was hit by a cyclone many years before and when grandpa was taking a nap, the wind removed the roof. He didn't hear a thing.

My grandmother solved the problem about the radio. I had found a real good short wave radio and at her suggestion we hid it under my bed and my dear grandpa never knew the difference. He couldn't hear a thing!

He loved to play checkers, as long as he won. For many years he received $100 a month for being a Civil War Veteran. He could have had more but he said it was enough to live on. When the weather was permissible, he would walk about two blocks to town every day. Sometimes he would stop to visit with Judge Miller, an old army friend. One grapefruit a day was his policy. He always had a garden and buried his garbage. He knew the value of a compost.

The years 1934 and 35 were tough. Try as I could, I couldn't find a job. In desperation I joined the National Guard, a machine gun outfit. Little did I know that the only way to get out was to move from the state. No one thought about war.

I did love target practice and got paid for it. We were called out once to Lincoln, Nebraska to stop a political riot. When the National Guard showed up, the riot ended. It proved the saying, "If you want peace, prepare for war." While there, I saw President Roosevelt just as the train was pulling out. He was standing at the back rail of the train waving his arms.

Not having a job didn't set very well with my grandfather. I guess he thought I was lazy. He never knew about unemployment, as he was a self-employed carpenter. He voted for F.D.R. but regretted it later. He never could understand why the government paid the farmer for not growing wheat.

Finally, a neighbor opened a factory and advised me to apply for a job, which I did, picking feathers off of chickens, a very prestigious job. One chicken at a time and to make any kind of money I had to make those feathers fly. What a job. It made my grandpa happy, but I never told him what I did.

But that job soon became tiresome and I had a chance to work in a greenhouse. Whenever there was a funeral I had to work in the floral shop making sprays. As it turned out there was a funeral almost every day so I didn't spend much time in the greenhouse. First thing in the morning I would help make sprays and floral baskets. We got roses from Denver and gladiolus from Oklahoma. In those days the body would first be taken to the home, then to the church and then to the cemetery. My job was to take the flowers first, to the home, arrange them, open the coffin, and put a rose in the hands of the deceased, which made me feel a little squeamish. Then I had to make sure I got the flowers to the church before the people got there and lastly to the cemetery.

The first car I owned was a Ford Coupe. The tag cost 50 cents. When business was slow in the greenhouse I would vaccinate pigs, a sideline my boss had. Refrigerators were scarce in those days. The only one in town was in the Floral Shop. That is the reason my boss vaccinated pigs. The serum had to be refrigerated.

My uncle Charley Hedges, my father's brother, lived in Seward and my mother's sister, Aunt Emma Findley and family lived in Beaver-Crossing, near Seward. I had many cousins and we were together on weekends.

1936 was the first year that "LIFE" magazine published their first issue. It arrived in the newsstand in November and sold for 10 cents.

1936 also closed this chapter of my life. Things are always changing.

Chapter 6

Cambridge, Wisconsin

My sister Grace and her husband, Selmer, lived in Chicago with their three young children, Daytha, Alice, and Wesley. Selmer managed the Goodwill Industries in Chicago. When he became ill, Mr. Don Prescott, an old friend of the family, invited them to stay in his cottage at Lake Ripley near Cambridge, Wisconsin. Selmer had grown up in Cambridge where his father had been a pastor at the oldest Scandinavian Methodist Church in the world. They came, but a few months later Selmer died and my sister moved to a house in Cambridge. I received a stressful letter from Grace asking me to come and stay with her.

There was no question about it. I didn't have to go, but I wanted to. Grace and Selmer were very special to me. Selmer taught me how to drive a car and he helped me through my high school years and gave me much spiritual encouragement. I said good-bye to Nebraska. I was released from the Nebraska National Guard. Wisconsin here I come!

My model A Ford Coupe barely made it to Wisconsin. It was old when I got it and it had served me well, but now, as an Italian would say, finito! I bought a new 1936 Plymouth Sedan for $800.

If I thought 1934 and 1935 were tough years, 1936 was even worse. We discovered the baker in Cambridge wanted to sell the bakery. With her insurance money, Grace bought the bakery and the baker promised to stay and teach us. We had no experience in baking. A neighbor woman back on the farm had taught me how to make baking powder biscuits. Grace, while in Minneapolis, worked one night in a bakery and got fired for burning the pies.

But Grace excelled at making cookies, cakes, and pies. Bread, sweet rolls, danish, and doughnuts, were my specialties. A year later we bought a 1937 Dodge truck and I delivered bread to several small towns.

After graduating from high school in Seward, June 1937, my sister Eunice came to Cambridge to help in the bakery. Shortly after that a young German baker came in looking for work. The baker we had, had other plans so we hired the young German. His name was Kurt Holzinger. It wasn't long until Eunice and Kurt fell in love and were married in 1938. Kurt became a welcome member of the family. I learned a lot from Kurt, but after he thought we could manage the baking, he bought his own bakery in Fort Atkinson, a town near Cambridge.

Cambridge, a quaint little town with umbrellas up and down Main Street is noted for its fine pottery factory and is a haven for tourists. It is located a couple of miles from the famous Lake Ripley where many people from Chicago have their summer homes. The Methodist Church owned a Bible Camp on the lake and gave the bakery a lot of business. Every week a different group would rent the campgrounds to hold meetings and camp for the young people. One group I liked very much was the Grace Gospel Fellowship. I heard great Bible teachers like J. C.O'Hair, C. R. Stam, and

Charles Baker. Through their teaching and writing I learned there is but one true Bible church in this dispensation; the Body of Christ, which was not revealed in other ages. There is only one way to be saved, by grace through faith in the crucified and glorified Christ. Members of Christ's Body are delivered from religion as well as from the law of Sinai and the law of sin and death. It was a turning point in my Christian life.

Several people from Madison, a short distance from Cambridge, enjoyed our baking and one woman in particular gave us orders and wanted me to deliver.

One day when delivering a large order to this woman's house, I heard over the radio that Hitler had invaded Poland, 1939, the beginning labor pains of World War II. It didn't enter my mind that I would be affected by a war in Poland.

I worked in the bakery for five years, a struggle at times but I enjoyed it, especially helping my sister. I made many lasting friends in Cambridge, especially Ellis Mooney, who spent hours trying to teach me how to carry a tune. Finally, he gave up in despair. He went to college and became a youth pastor in Sheboygan, Wisconsin. Ardell Jarsberg and Ruth Kenseth were two good friends from the Methodist church but nothing serious.

In 1937 my Grandpa Creighton died and Mother returned to Minneapolis. She stayed with my brother Elmer, and his wife Violet, and their two sons, Barton, and James. Barton, my nephew, wrote me a letter telling me about my mother. "I certainly remember Grandma Hedges staying at our house. I was ten years old. She was ailing with an arthritis that affected her skin. I recall she couldn't close her hands; her skin was so tight. She stayed with us about a year spending some time at Uncle Lewis and Aunt Ruby's. She was such a good sport. We played Chinese checkers by the hour and she had it down to a science. I don't remember her being bed-ridden but she had a hard time getting around by herself. I remember her shawl and knit slippers and her worn Bible with our Lord's words printed in red. She was a remarkable lady to survive Kansas and

Minnesota and to keep her faith through her losses. My dad (Elmer) was the last child born in the sod house in Colby, Kansas."

They gave her much tender and loving care. Mother died on Mother's Day May 14, 1939, three years before I was drafted in to the U.S Army.

***

December 7, 1941

***

Sunday morning, December 7th, 1941, while eating breakfast a neighbor boy, Donny Prescott Jr., came dashing to my house shouting hysterically, "Guess what? Japan just bombed Pearl Harbor."

Three days later, December 10th, Hitler declared war on the United States.

My first notice from Uncle Sam said, "deferred because of my age." The second notice, 6 months later, I was deferred because I was supporting my sister and family. In 3 more months the third notice said, "We need you! Report to Madison, at once for your physical."

While standing in line, for a physical examination, stripped of all clothing, I still thought I would be deferred, but the doctor soon changed my mind. He said, "Yours is the best sounding heart I have heard all day."

I just turned 31. Once again another chapter in my life came to a close.

Chapter 7

Zigzagging across The Atlantic

In two weeks, after saying good-bye, I went to Milwaukee, Wisconsin for my basic training.

Stella Lillison a friend of the family gave me a Gideon Bible and wrote in it; "Safety does not depend on the absence of danger, but on the presence of "The Lord." A truth I experienced many times.

After a month of close-order drill, K P, and guard duty in Milwaukee, I received official notice of my attachment to the 15th Evacuation Hospital, as the baker. It was located at Fort Meade, Maryland.

My arrival to Fort Meade happened one rainy night at midnight and my introduction to the kitchen where I would do my baking turned out to be rather creepy. When the lights went on, I never saw so many healthy cockroaches at one time run for their lives. The large hard wood table was covered with the critters, but in a few seconds they had all scampered between the cracks and crevices. I knew I was at war. My first assignment—get rid of the cockroaches!

While taking a shower one night I over heard two fellows in a very deep argument. One, a typical southerner from Virginia and the other had a very western drawl. The southerner, as I could figure out, sounded like a Southern Baptist and the other fellow talked like an agnostic. The point of the argument was, "could one believe the Bible?" After the discussion ended I went to the southern and told him I wasn't a Baptist but I agreed with him; "One could believe the Bible."

This was my first introduction to Craig Burleson who became my best friend.

Fort Meade was equal distance from Baltimore and Washington D. C. Many people from churches in Baltimore came to camp and invited the service men to their homes for Sunday dinner. Mrs. Rhodes invited Craig and me to dinner several times and promised to write to us.

Craig and I explored Washington D. C. together. My stay in Fort Meade lasted about six weeks and from there we went to Camp Kilmore, New Jersey. Camp Kilmore was a jumping off place for overseas duty. The night before we were to load on the ship I came down with a severe strep throat and there was danger that I would be left behind. It was unthinkable that I should be separated from my friends and outfit that I had grown accustomed to. I went to the dispensary and asked to have my throat coated with iodine. The nurse advised me it would hurt but after I insisted, she did it. The next morning I passed inspection, the iodine worked, and before the sun faded in to the night we were assigned to our bunks on a large troop ship.

I have no idea how many ships were in the convoy but for seven long weeks we zigzaged across the Atlantic. The reason for the zigzaging, as I could figure, was to avoid direct hits from German submarines.

Seven weeks sleeping on hammock like beds made my bones ache, not exactly a leisure trip. The captain ordered complete black outs at night. "Shut the door," became a byword. In the thick darkness you could feel a deep gloom, a sense of mystery, apprehension, and wonder. When would it end— and where?

The high winds caused large swells that tossed the ship up and down, but as we entered the Straits of Gibraltar the ocean suddenly became very calm. The calm water sparkled like silvery glass, not a sign of a ripple. The ship slowed down to a crawl. To add to the suspense a rumor went around that German submarines were in the vicinity. There was a full moon that made us a perfect target. I could feel the intensity of that moment. Through out the night a ghastly silence became our uninvited guest; no one was talking, not a whisper. I felt very much part of the scenery. I had no fear, while many were fearful. All through that night I knew a Mighty Hand stretched over our ship. It reminded me of the night the Death Angel passed over Israel in Egypt. Those who obeyed and put the sacrificial blood of the lamb over the doorpost were in complete safety. Early in the morning, as the sun appeared on the horizon, we could see an outline of land. Before high noon, we disembarked at Oran, North Africa.

Oran, a seaport, certainly was a strange city and full of contrasts. The mixture of so many races living together with all of their differences, languages, and customs, dazzled me. The natives lived very close together even with the animals and not much thought was given to sanitation. Six times a day, bells rang and Moslems bowed down to the ground facing the East.

To see the different means of travel was very amusing. The large and swift GI Army trucks seemed out of place among the wooden carts the natives used. I never saw any two carts alike. There were no standard models, all shapes and sizes, drawn by mules, donkeys, and horses, on which you could count every rib. Oh yes, I forgot the charcoal trucks that create their own gas and usually have to stop half way up the hill to get enough power to make the grade. Once in awhile you would see a first class buggy.

The French and Spanish dressed fairly nice, but the poorer class of Arabs wore anything they could get their hands on. Rags, some discarded garment, sacks, and sheets, made up their wearing apparel, if they were lucky to get that much. One day I saw a fine young gentleman proudly walking down Main Street with nothing on except a pair of G.I. heavy underwear. I am sure he thought he was well dressed; compared to some of the others, he was..

We camped about two miles from Oran. For excitement we could go into town. I became acquainted with a French-Jewish family. They invited me to their home for dinner several times. Talk about French cuisine! I didn't remember the names of the different dishes but they were good!

My friends were giving me a tour of the city when we came to a building that kindled my curiosity. They insisted I go in and they would wait for me outside. Very reluctantly I went to the large doors and was greeted by a very friendly Arab. First he insisted I take my shoes off. (I was told they had such a custom) Then he motioned for me to take off my shirt. This must be a very holy place! To please him I took off my shirt, then I drew the line. He wanted my watch and insisted I take off my pants and handed me a very large sheet. I very politely tried to tell him I was in a hurry and had to go. With a very surprised look, he watched me dress and I left the building. My friends were waiting for me. When I told them what happened they couldn't stop laughing. They thought I wanted a steam bath. I had no idea what I was getting in to. Come to think of it, people do take off their clothing for a steam bath!

Time went by and we still waited for orders to go into action. The evenings became very boring so the Chaplain decided to get the personnel together and sing the old time songs in the Army hymnal. No one volunteered to play the reed organ. I had played the organ a little and told the Chaplain that with some practice I would be able to play most of the hymns in the book. I spent most of my spare time practicing. Almost every night we would sing late into the night, singing the same songs over and over again. My legs got a good work out pumping the reed organ.

Many times in the late afternoon my friend Craig and I walked through the town of Oran. It was very depressing to see how the people lived. Women were cooking the evening meal over small fires along the streets. Nothing went to waste. Once I was offered the guts and intestines of chickens fried in olive oil. "Very good," I was told. For some reason I lost my appetite. Food was scarce for these people and they had to use every bit of their wit just to survive. Naked children stood around the make shift outdoor kitchens waiting to be fed, but they barely got enough to keep them alive. They did have some fruit. The Army personnel were forbidden to eat any food or fruit in town because of sanitary reasons.

The days were hot, but the nights were bitter cold. We were told to get used to shaving in cold water, a habit I soon became accustomed to, reluctantly.

Waiting for marching orders sometimes seems more difficult than regular combat. The unknown causes anxious moments. Even in the center of action we knew very little of what was really happening.

We read about it later. Sometimes the Army newspaper would catch up with us. Many days after the action, we discovered some of the events that had taken place.

Hitler won the race against Eisenhower to seize Tunisia, but it was short-lived victory. American troops under Eisenhower hit the beaches of Morocco and Algeria on November 8, 1942. The Germans retreated and this was the time we (the 15th Evacuation Hospital) landed in Oran.

Brigadier General Erin Rommel was in command of the Italian-German force in North Africa. He had made a name for himself as commander of a Panzer division in the battle of France. He proved to be a gigantic problem to the British in the North African desert; a problem that lasted for two years. The British were loosing control. When the Allied Forces pushed Rommel from Africa, they never retreated again. They were always on the move forward until the recapture of France and Germany.

Roosevelt's New Deal was not too popular in 1940. Hitler took advantage of this and tried to cause division in American politics, through his endless propaganda. He accused Roosevelt of starting the war and everything else that he himself was guilty of. But after Pearl Harbor, the whole country came to the support of their country. Pearl Harbor was a small victory for Japan. However, it unified the American people and Japan had wakened a sleeping giant.

Hitler knew exactly what he wanted; a Nazi ruled Europe. The people of these countries would be slaves to the Master Race and all undesirable elements especially the Jews would be exterminated. Hitler declared there should be one Master. " Two masters side by side cannot and must not exist. We are the Master Race and must govern hard but just. I did not come to spread bliss. The population must work, work, and work again. We definitely did not come here to give out manna."

Hitler should have learned his lesson from past history. God had declared way back in the biblical record of Genesis and Exodus that He had a plan for the nation of Israel. Many have tried to destroy Israel but never succeeded. The Oracle of God still stands. The prophecy has yet to be fulfilled, but will be in the coming age. Many have tried to destroy the Jews to their own destruction.

The subject of the Jews is a phenomenon. Because of their disobedience it was foretold they would be scattered to all points of the earth. No matter where you go you will find the Jews; not true of any other race.

At least Hitler was honest when he said he did not come to spread bliss or to give manna. He lost it all.

"What does it profit a man if he gains the whole world and looses his own soul?"

On the other hand, according to the biblical account, Christ came to seek and to save that which is lost. "Come unto me," he said "and I will give you rest." Instead of taking life, He gave His life.

The leaders of the nation of Israel rejected the offer of the King and the Kingdom. Because of their rejection, God temporarily set them aside.

On the road to Damascus, God saved Saul whose name was changed to Paul. The Lord said, "This man is my chosen instrument to carry my name before the Gentiles and their kings and before the people of Israel." Through the Apostle Paul, The Resurrected and Glorified Christ, revealed to him the dispensation or administration of Grace, the present time in which we are living. When this dispensation is ended and the Church, the Body of Christ, is completed and removed from the earth, God will again deal with the Nation of Israel. God will take them through the great tribulation and then Christ will come back and Israel will again become a nation. A Nation will be born in a day.

Poor Hitler…he was ignorant of God's prophecy concerning the Jews. Yes, Hitler killed many of them but could not eliminate them.

Waiting six long weeks at Oran for our marching orders we had time to think. It became a time of reflection on the politics of the day, trying to understand the times we lived in. The reason for the campaign in North Africa, we decided, was to protect the Suez Canal. The Canal was Britain's lifeline to India and the Far East. In the desert, victory went to the side with the most gasoline.

Finally the orders came and we were on the move. Each time we set up the tents as though we would be permanent, but in a few days or less we would move again. We were within the sound of guns and were the first to care for the wounded. On such occasions I would do no baking, instead I would help the medics care for the patients.

The 15th Evacuation Hospital came to Oran at the time when the American and British forces were at a tug of war with Rommel, the so-called "Desert Fox." After several advances and retreats the Germans were forced to Algeria and Tunisia, and then to Sicily. Slowly we made our way to Bizerte, a city that was completely destroyed. Nothing but rubble, not a building was standing. From Bizerte we crossed the Mediterranean Sea to Gela, Sicily. Because we were an evacuation hospital, we were constantly on the move.

Carrigan, a friend, made a cartoon for the Army newspaper. It featured a picture of Mussolini and Hitler in a tub looking the worse for wear. Mussolini is looking through a telescope and Hitler asks, "See anything behind us, old pucker lip?" Mussolini replies, "The 15th Evac are putting up their tents so the infantry and artillery can't be far behind."

In Gela we witnessed an after effect of a fierce tank battle, one disaster after another. The countryside was covered with tangled barbed wire, destroyed machine-gun emplacements, shattered tanks, and fallen bodies. After a battle there is a very distinct odor of dead bodies and gun smoke. It gives one a very eerie feeling. But after the battle you could always hear birds singing and the fields would be covered with wild flowers.

From Gela we went to Caltanissetta and then on to Palermo, the first European city to be liberated. I witnessed Mt. Etna in action. The air looked like ghostly clouds trimmed in burning red. It really was dormant, but at night the fire and smoke rises heavenward above the snow-capped mountains making a spectacular sight. The last eruption happened in 1955 when many people perished. The soil around the base of the volcano is very fertile, an incentive to live and farm there. The base spreads out a hundred miles to the Mediterranean Sea.

Early one morning we packed all of our worldly possessions into tight bundles and loaded them on large amphibious "Ducks" that had been assigned to carry the personnel of the 15th Evacuation Hospital.

The "Duck" was another American innovation. No other country had anything to compare to it. It could carry twenty fully equipped riflemen in combat. Those oversized boats with wheels had padded seats and were fairly comfortable. I sympathized with the poor souls that had dysentery. For them the ride was unbearable. It slowed us down because we had to stop so many times. The road from Palermo to Messina follows the coast and is every picturesque. The high cliffs and long tunnels through the mountains gives a thrill of a lifetime, especially the winding roads. Many curves were so sharp the "Ducks" would have to stop and back up to swing around the bend. Even the small GI jeeps would have to maneuver around the cures. The U.S. "jeep" was the envy of the world's armies. Wherever America fought, the "jeep" was there. We arrived in Messina just at dusk and only caught a glimpse of Messina's artistic buildings. We camped on a vacant lot and in the morning we were up at 4:30, and waited until late afternoon before we crossed the Strait of Messina. There is a saying in the Army, "hurry up and wait," which we experienced many times.

On the eventful day of October 22, 1943, I set foot on the mainland of Italy.

As we traveled up the boot of Italy in the same "Ducks" through many small towns and villages as invaders, the people greeted us joyfully, handing out fruit, flowers, and wine. The children threw us hot roasted chestnuts and boy, did they ever taste good! The people treated us more like "liberators" instead of "invaders." Many of the American soldiers who had Italian heritage and spoke the language fluently looked for long lost relatives. It was a time of rejoicing for the Italian people, even though most of the country was still in the grip of the German army. The hearts of the Italian people didn't want war; they surrendered willingly.

Finally we camped in Alife, a small town outside of Naples. I never saw so much mud! It rained and the heavy trucks cut deep furrows in the water soaked earth. We couldn't keep the mud out of our pup tents. The mud was like glue at midday and like iron in the freezing nights. While we were waiting for our next move, we had a few days to explore Naples, Pompeii, and Mount Vesuvious.

Naples is the third largest city of Italy, has great beauty mixed with crowded slums. Naples lies amid some of the most spectacular scenery in Europe. Mount Vesuvious can be seen in the distance. The Neapolitans are carefree and always singing but watch out for the pickpockets. They are clever by getting your attention and rob you blind. Riding on a crowded streetcar once I had my wristwatch stolen. Never-the-less Naples, is a fun city and everybody sings "O Sole Mio."

Pompeii, an ancient city in Italy, disappeared when Mount Vesuvious erupted in AD 79; rediscovered in 1700. Pompery the Great-106-48BC was an outstanding Roman general. He was the obstacle in the rise of power of Julius Caesar.

Mount Vesuvious is the only active volcano on the mainland of Europe. It is near the Bay of Naples, 7 miles southeast of Naples, erupts frequently and is easy to reach. Ash from Vesuvious has made the soil extremely fertile. The finest grapes are grown there. I was in Florence when the last eruption happened in 1944.

At Alife I met Sisto Zeppetelli, a fourteen-year old Italian boy. Ernie Monseni, an Army buddy, and I spent many happy hours with Sisto and his family.

Sisto

The bombing had partially destroyed their home. They seemed to have plenty of beans and could they ever make them taste good. Their good olive oil was the secret. Sisto's mother was very thin and so sad. The war was hard on her. They had experienced chaos, devastation, terror, and destruction but in spite of it all they were happy to be alive and no one in the family was hurt.

Chapter 8

ANZIO

Our rest didn't last long at Alife. A hospital had been accidentally bombed at Anzio and we replaced it. Anzio came close to being a complete disaster. The surprised Germans had time to mass troops and artillery; they almost succeeded wiping out the beachhead.

Most of the American troops that landed at Anzio were fresh out of high school; as one reporter said, "They arrived as innocent kids; after a day or two of combat they became veterans." There was no way the Army could have prepared them for this. The whine of the Artillery sounded like the scream of a mad-person. It was cold; trench foot, and frostbite were common. It was Italy's worst winter in decades. A great number suffered from shell shock. Foxholes filled with rainwater; the only protection came from sand bags and a few buildings that had not been smashed to complete rubble. Usually the Germans respected the Red Cross, that is, the hospitals, but many times the artillery shells would fall short of their intended destination. Fortunately for us many of the shells that fell in the hospital area were duds, and buried themselves in the sand, thanks to some saboteurs in German factories.

One patient we had was badly injured in his legs and gangrene had set in. He was given a choice, to have his legs amputated or try a new medicine. The new medicine was penicillin, the first time it was used in the Army. It not only saved the soldier's life but also his legs. Penicillin was discovered in1928 but not perfected until 1944.

One time when Ernie Munseni and I were investigating a damaged unit we saw cameramen taking pictures. We had no idea who they were. Later I received a letter from home saying they saw my picture in "Life Magazine," June 1944.

There were no shortages of dogfights in mid air and flares by night. Whether it was a German or Allied plane that burst into flames, spin out of control, and crashed to the ground in a trail of smoke, I would say a prayer for the pilot. Sometimes a parachute saved his life. In a short time I could distinguish between the sound of the Luftwaffe (German) and the B-29 (American).

The Germans had literally buried themselves in rock at Cassino. Anzio was between Rome and Cassino. The purpose of Anzio was to divide the German army. Leaflets signed by Roosevelt and Churchill were dropped over Rome and other cities, stating, "Decide—-die for Mussolini and Hitler—-or live for Italy and civilization." Mussolini became the most hated man in Italy. It was a long and costly struggle; the Allied Forces prevailed. The "Jerries," (a reference to the German soldiers) finally retreated past Rome.

The Allies were on the move and the 15th Evacuation Hospital once more broke camp and set up in Rome for a much needed rest. After effects of a great stress can be devastating. We had many replacements due to mental breakdown and physical fatigue. The noise was the worst for me. The bursting shells went straight to my bones.

The fall of Rome marked the beginning of the last phase of the European war. Two days later, Eisenhower's force landed in Normandy.

Our stay in Rome lasted two weeks, but I did have time to explore the catacombs, some of the ancient ruins, and St. Peter's Church. The catacombs were used as burial places in Rome. The early Christians used them as secret meeting places. Saint Peter's Basilica located in Vatican City in the shape of a cross. The architectural feature is its magnificent dome, designed by Michelangelo. Constantine the Great started building the church in 325 and it was completed in 1667.

We read in the Army newspaper about a doughboy that made the classic remark when he saw the ruins of the Colesseum, "Gee, I didn't know our bombers had done that much damage in Rome."

One experience I had in Rome, I remember with amusement. I became friends with a patient by the name of Hershey. We would take long walks; we both needed the exercise. During our walks I noticed a man following us. The first couple of times I didn't think much about it, just my runaway imagination. I didn't want to mention it to my friend as he was recovering from shell shock. It happened again, the same man lagging behind us. This time my friend noticed my concern. He said, "Don't mind him," referring to the man, "he thinks I am somebody else."

I really was confused now. He went on further trying to explain. "The Army is always getting me mixed up with another patient whose name is Hershey. The other Hershey is heir to the Hershey Chocolate fortune and his family has body guards where ever he goes."

Well, that settled the mystery, or did it? I never knew for sure if he was telling me the truth or if he was the real "Hershey."

Chapter 9

Romance in Florence

No matter where we were, we always received V-Mail, little letters that could reach even the most outlandish destination in about ten days.

We finally reached the beautiful city of Florence. In Florence the 15th Evac became a general hospital where we stayed in one place and patients came to us for recovery. We never acted as an evacuation hospital again.

It was late in the afternoon when we arrived in Florence, dead tired. We put up our tents on the grounds of a Catholic seminary. A high stonewall surrounded the grounds, with a large iron gate at the entrance. It looked more like a prison. There were buildings to house the patients, doctors, and nurses, but the rest of the personnel stayed in tents. After all that traveling my clothes were dirty, and I needed a hot shower.

Wherever we went, Italian boys and girls were curious to see us and to make friends. They loved chewing gum and "caramelle." One twelve year old boy came to me, not for gum like the rest, but said his mother would "wash" my clothes if I would furnish "Sapone" (soap). That sounded like a good deal so I gave the boy all the clothes I had except the ones I had on. Craig chided me that I would never see my clothes again. The boy looked honest and I knew the people needed soap and I decided to take the chance. I did ask for his name and address. His name was "Andrea" and he lived just a short distance from the hospital.

Two and three days went by and no clothes. The fourth day I decided I better investigate. Craig and I took a walk to see if we could find such a number. As we walked down the street I saw Andrea coming toward us carrying my clothes. With him, were his mother, a five-year-old brother, Guido, and his twenty -year old sister, Teresa, whose nickname was " Cina." My clothes were immaculately cleaned and pressed. I became the best-dressed GI in the Fifth Army. We were closer to their apartment than to the hospital, so they invited us to their home. It greatly relieved me to have the only clothes I owned safely back and my friend conceded I was a good judge of human nature. Sure enough, such a number existed.

We had a delightful time getting acquainted with Andrea and his family. We also met his father, a very stately man but just a little dubious of American soldiers. The German soldiers pillaged and raped when retreating.

Andrea's mother decided to make some espresso coffee and some how a fire got started and filled the apartment with smoke. We soon put the fire out and we could breath again. My attention centered on Cina. I believed my heart stopped beating once or twice. She could speak English; just needed a little practice, and I could practice with her, very willingly. I had found my dream girl, but to make matters worse she seemed to fall for Craig's southern drawl. She loved to hear him say, "Finito Benito."

Craig and I were on duty and had to return to camp. What excuse could I think of to see her again; more dirty clothes? Funny we should meet over some dirty laundry, just one of those little things. As we went out the door, Cina said, "Come and see us whenever you can." Whoopee! That was what I wanted to hear.

That's how it started. Nick, another friend, Craig and I went down to their house as often as we could get away. Sometimes I would take the reed organ that folded up like a suitcase and we would sing hymns.

Cina's father said he didn't like American music. His love was opera and knew most of them by heart. Living at the time of Caruso, he had the opportunity to sing in his choral group, but turned it down, because he wouldn't travel and leave his family. It wasn't long until he loved the hymns and would hum along with us. Craig and Nick were good singers and I played the organ. This went on for several weeks. Sometimes when we couldn't get a pass we would crawl over the stonewall and sneak down a dark alley to Cina's house. I had a sympathetic mess sergeant. Sometimes when the truck went to the quartermaster for food, we stopped by Cina's house and left all of the old grease from frying doughnuts. They used it to make soap.

One eventful night when all three of us were there, when we were leaving, Cina took me aside and asked if I could come down alone. I assured her I would and sealed it with a kiss, or two.

Crawling over the stonewall at night and walking down a dark alley, all alone, was scary; but nothing could stop me from seeing my dream girl. An American soldier courting an Italian beauty didn't set well with the local young men. Cina's family at that time didn't have electricity so I would bring some candles, the largest I could find, and her father would say, "Finito candle," time to go home!

In Florence my "Bakery" operated at full force. Our personnel plus the patients made our hospital a small village. I had good help. Clyde Brooks was my assistant and I had an Italian prisoner of war as a helper. Two enterprising young men who had newspaper experience started a weekly paper for the hospital. They called their paper "The Scalpel." On March 2, 1945 the bakery made the front page. The headlines—-THE BAKING UNIT—-"After two years of industrious enterprise, the Hedges and

Brooks Baking Co., has finally begun to show a profit. The management wishes to take this opportunity to wish all of you who have faithfully patronized their humble shop, to inspect their new modernized plant. Since they closed the old bakery on Mud Lane near the old motor pool site, a new and larger tent has been erected with all the latest improvements to safeguard your health and please your palate. Among the improvements made in the new bakery is a rebuilt oven. The unit is in excellent repair, and all should go well. We can expect more, and even better delicacies in the future." (Note to Editor: This article netted me exactly one cream-puff. —Jake)

The baker had an advantage over the cooks. No matter how hard they tried the cooks couldn't make dried egg powder to taste like an egg benedict or fluffy scrambled eggs. On the other hand, I could use the dreaded dried eggs to make delicious homemade doughnuts, cookies, pies, and cakes, which would bring a touch of home. I received special treatment from the personnel. The cooks were famous for their good coffee—a cup of coffee and a fresh doughnut brought memories of home.

In the weeks that followed I spent all of my spare time with Cina going to Museums, cathedrals, and art galleries. Things were going great. Just one draw back, Cina was already engaged. She didn't agree with her fiancé's philosophy; an avowed atheist and she was a devout Catholic and to make matters worse I was a devout Protestant. I gave Cina the first Bible she ever read, the little Gideon New Testament with Psalms and Proverbs that was given to me when I entered the Army. She loved to read it and memorized many of the Psalms.

Cina decided to give me a good education in Italian Art, something I sorely lacked. What did I know about the Renaissance or the Patti and the Medici Families? Yes, I had heard of Michelangelo, Leonardo da Vinci, and the Aaron River —the extent of my knowledge of Florentine history. I knew Michelangelo was a great artist and sculptor and if I remember correctly, he painted the Sistine Chapel. But what did I know about Art? Cina exposed me to Italian culture. The first time around Palazzo Della

Signori, I confess, I was rather confused, but gradually I began to enjoy it and looked forward to viewing the Uffizi Gallery.

The Germans destroyed most of the ancient bridges of Florence when they were retreating in 1944, however the Ponte Vecchio (the famous old bridge) still stands undamaged. My favorite place was the Gallery of the Academy, where Michelangelo's David is in a large room with sun light overhead; the sun's rays give an added dimension. It makes you feel like a midget beside this huge marble statue of the biblical Shepherd Boy. The statue is awesome and it looks like it could come to life at any moment, a masterpiece in sculpturing. I have seen many copies of "The David" but none compare with the original.

I like the way the guide described the statue.

"You sense the young David who is to fight the great Goliath, having confidence in God, capable of winning and already victorious. You sense the restrained majesty, a super-human power, the knitted brow and those eyes, concentrated on the task ahead."

Life seemed great. I had completely fallen in love with this beautiful, charming, graceful, young Italian girl with a radiant smile. But, as I said before, there was one drawback; she was already engaged.

One sunny afternoon Cina and I planned to meet in front of the Cathedral of Santa Maria del Fiore (the Duomo). On my way, I passed a floral shop and purchased a large bouquet of flowers, just the right thing to do to express my growing love for her. When we met, Cina's fiancé showed up with his mother at the same time. How could I give the flowers to Cina in front of her fiancé? It was an awkward situation for me so I had to think fast. Cina introduced me to this fine Italian lady who was related to Cina's uncle by marriage. She seemed so pleased to meet me that I presented her with the lovely bouquet of roses. She received them with enthusiasm, especially coming from an American soldier. We did some small talk and treated ourselves to a cup of espresso coffee and then I excused myself because suddenly I remembered I was due at the camp.

Cina's fiancé was a good artist and had given her many beautiful paintings. He treated me very friendly, I thought it strange because Cina and I were together a lot; he wasn't worried about me, it was my good friend Nick that he had his eye on. He was the handsome one and he figured that Cina might fall for him.

Cina and I continued to go for long walks whenever I had time off. There was always something new to see. We climbed to the top of the Duomo with its very small steps, falling deeper in love with each step.

It wasn't long until her fiancé became suspicious and laid down the law. Cina could not see me anymore and he wanted to get married right away. Before, he said he would never marry her until she had a dowry.

The Chaplain of the hospital asked us three (Craig, Nick and I) if we would hold services for the patients during the week. Nick became the song leader, Craig the speaker and I played the organ. Cina loved to sing and would come to the hospital for the services. One evening Cina and her mother came to visit. I was playing the organ and Nick was leading the singing when Cina's fiancé came storming in the chapel looking for Cina. He had fire in his eyes and determined to put a stop to this nonsense. Before he could start a rumpus, Cina and her mother very quietly and quickly went to him and took him by the arm and led him out of the room to avoid a commotion. We very nervously carried on the service.

After the service, I went to Cina's to see what happened. There was an argument. He slapped Cina in the face. That was enough to call off the engagement. He had given Cina some very beautiful paintings and demanded that she return everything he had given her. To start with she gave him back the engagement ring and then the slap in the face that he had just given to her. Cina paid for some of the paintings that she kept. One picture he wouldn't accept. It was a picture of a cat; an eloquent picture, however he was superstitious and refused to take it back but he sold it to her for ten lire.

Cina, for the first time, confessed to me that she wasn't really happy with the engagement; it lacked something that engaged people should have. I reached out to comfort her but we both knew it was more than just comfort, it was a bond that words can't describe, we were deeply in love.

Craig and I decided to go to every church in town to see if we could find one to our liking. We went to the Church of England, Methodist, Pentecostal, and some others besides the Catholic Church. Finally, we heard of a little church way across town. At that time during the war there were no streetcars or taxicabs, so we had to walk. It turned out to be a Waldensian Church, a name we had never heard of before. The Waldenses had close fellowship with the French Huguenots. In 1945 the Protestant Church was restricted in their freedom, no advertising of any kind. When the Allies took over Florence, General Mark Clark gave religious freedom to all churches. The Waldensian Church was named after Peter Waldo who lived at the time of Saint Francis of Assisi four hundred years before Martin Luther. We decided to visit this church with a strange name.

The Pastor spoke in Italian but we could recognize the songs. The congregation sang like a choir, all singing the different parts, beautiful harmony. The Pastor spoke in Italian but we knew he was preaching from Romans, a book from the New Testament. "Solo Fede" we understood. (Faith only) This was the church we were looking for.

We made a deal with Cina. One Sunday we would go to her church and then she would visit this little church we had found.

The next Sunday, Cina, her mother, Andrea, Guido, Craig, and I, started walking to the church of our choice. After walking for a long time, Cina's mother decided for certain we were lost. Cina said she knew of no such church on this street. We kept telling them "finito strada," at the end of the street. They didn't believe us until we finally found the door and walked in. Cina didn't commit herself if she enjoyed the service or not. She said nothing one way or the other.

The following Sunday, Craig and I went alone to the Waldensian Church, however, Cina insisted we come to her house for dinner after church.

The Pastor could speak English and on our way out we told him how much we enjoyed the service. I also mentioned Cina, the Italian girl, and wished that sometime he could meet her. He said he would be happy to. When we arrived at Cina's home, dinner was ready and we enjoyed pasta, Italian style.

During the week Cina and I visited more art galleries and the neat little restaurants along the narrow streets. The lunch counter at the train station specialized in Tortelini, which was fabulous. We went to the Florence Opera House; my first opera was Madame Butterfly. It changed my preconceived idea about opera. Instead of being boring, it captivated me. The music, the sound, the acting overwhelmed me. When Madame Butterfly committed Hara Kiri I thought it was real. Another opera we saw was La Traviata, very lively music. I fell in love with Verde's music.

The next Sunday, Cina said she would go with us to church and then she told us what happened the Sunday before. She did go to church by bicycle, arriving late and sat way in the back row. After the service she wanted to speak to the Pastor. She hid in a little room at the rear of the church and overheard me telling the Pastor about the "Italian girl" I wanted him to meet. She then hurried home on her bicycle and arrived long before we did. Cina expressed to the Pastor how much she enjoyed hearing the Word of God and asked if he could teach her more. The Pastor was more then willing. During the week he came to her house, first he went through the book of John, then to the letters of the Apostle Paul. She soon learned from the Word of God that there is only one true church, the Body of Christ. Christ is the head and all true believers are members regardless of what denomination they belong to. There is only one God who created heaven and earth and has revealed Himself in the person of God the Son, Christ Jesus the Lord. None of us deserve to be saved and He saves us by His divine Grace, just because we believe the record God has given of His Son. *Ephesians 1:7 "In whom we have redemption through His blood, the forgiveness of sins, according to the riches of His Grace".*

***

1945

***

The German empire collapsed and the war in Europe came to a screeching halt; Hitler went down in defeat! Big headlines in the Army Newspaper;

THE WAR IN EUROPE IS OVER!

Cina's father gave me his permission to marry his daughter. I couldn't speak Italian and he couldn't speak English but we understood each other perfectly. Now I had the difficult task of getting the approval of the Fifth Army. First I pleaded with the captain, then the colonel, and there were more forms to fill out.

The rumor was that the 15th Evac would be going to France, but instead we moved to Milan in northern Italy. Cina could come to the states only as my wife; it was imperative we get married before leaving Italy. The 5th Army made it very difficult to get married, especially in a foreign country. They realized in many cases it is a fly-by-night affair so the Army discourages such marriages. It became a crucial decision for me. My good friend, Craig settled the question, "If you have no doubts, go for it!" I had no doubts so I made another visit to the colonel. I think my mess sergeant; Sgt. Carl Eberhart convinced the colonel that this marriage was for real. In two days my permit came through. Lt. Clark, the Mess Officer, informed me he would make arrangements to fly me back to Florence as soon as I set the date.

I called the pastor of the Waldensian Church in Florence. It would take a couple of days to get proper authority in Florence. Pastor Vinay assured me he would have everything ready and we could get married in the church on Wednesday August 1st, 1945 at 5:00p.m.

Since Craig was my best friend, he became my best man. Lt. Clark kept his word and Craig and I flew back to Florence in an Army plane from Milan.

The young people of the church out did themselves. They decorated the church and it became a garden overnight. Now for rings! I tried in several stores but could find nothing. Finally I settled on brass rings. Remember, things are different in wartime. A wedding cake was out of the question. The pastor stayed up all night making apple doughnuts. Pina, a friend of Cina's played Handel's Largo from "Xerxes" on the organ. The bride and groom sat on two chairs facing the Pastor as he preformed the ceremony; which is an Italian custom. The congregation sang and the Pastor gave a short message. After the wedding, the reception consisted of delicious homemade apple doughnuts and coffee. Cina's uncle made arrangements for a taxie-cab and reservations at a local hotel. Cina's mother kept saying "rest camp" and "take it easy." I wonder what she meant? That night at the hotel we had the largest T-bone steak I ever ate.

Lt. Clark made arrangements for Cina, Craig and me to return to Milano in an Army truck. Somehow, someone managed to get a sofa in back of the truck and we had limousine service. A friend of the Pastor's had an apartment in Milan we could use as they were out of town. They were Jewish and were hiding from the Nazi. Pastor Vinay had helped a number of Jewish people during the war.

***

August 7, 1945
***

The atomic bomb was dropped on Hiroshima 6 days after we were married. It was the beginning of the end of the war in the Pacific.

At the end of the month there came good news and bad news. The good news was in a few days I would be going to Naples to board a ship back to the states to be discharged from the Army. The bad news, I would be separated from my beloved wife. The Red Cross assured me she would join me in a few weeks.

From Milan to Naples the 15th Evacuation Hospital went by Army trucks and we would be going through Florence. Cina rode with me in the convoy as far as Florence and it came time to say good-bye!

How do you say good-bye to someone you love? Separations are never easy. One moment I would have her in my arms and then a kiss and then a wave of the hand and I faded in the distance. Standing at the back of the truck my eyes were fastened on a beautiful, courageous and dynamic Italian girl who became my wife. She was no longer in sight. My eyes could not see her but I had her locked in my heart, and she was for real. She became the center of my life, more then I had hoped for in a wife, and she trusted me completely.

Was I really married? How did this Kansas boy manage to find this jewel in ancient Florence? I remembered my 12th birthday as I shot the arrow into the bull's eye. This is the girl that would change my life forever. How two people from two different cultures could find each other. Florence, Italy is half way around the world from Courtland, Kansas, truly a divine appointment.

I always had a great desire to be married and have a family of my own. Sometimes I would think the end of the world would come before my dream would come true. In my early manhood I promised the moon that when I, get married I would look up and say, "Thanks for the romance." It was like making a date with the moon. No, I didn't worship the moon but no matter where I went, the moon was always there. I could depend on it. As the truck vanished down the street leaving Florence, the moon was just peeking over the horizon. It was a full lonely red moon. With uplifted eyes I looked at the moon and said, "Thanks for the romance," and my heart was full of gratitude to my heavenly Father, who made the moon.

Cecchini Family 1945

Tais (Mother)

Guido (Father)

Cina

Andrea

Guido

Cina and Ernest

Cina in my uniform

Cina, Pastor Tuillo Vinay, and Ernest - Wedding day - August 1, 1945

Lt. Clark and Sgt. Eberhart

Ernest at the organ

Chapter 10

Honorable Discharge

Lonely is the only way I can describe my trip home on the boat. After moments of ecstasy and happiness, now I was without my dear wife. My heart felt totally empty. I had experienced a honeymoon beyond my fondest dreams. Life took on a new meaning; I would never be alone to dream, we could dream together. We were separated, but not in spirit. Leaving the calm waters of the Mediterranean and the Straits of Gibraltar, the great Atlantic looked threatening, nothing but darkness ahead. Carrigan and Ernie Monseni were two friends I spent a lot of time with. Craig went home on a different boat. We made our way to the bow of the ship and even though none of us could sing, we sang, "What a Friend We Have in Jesus." It was a song we knew well because we sang it a thousand times in

Algeria, North Africa. Carrigan was a great artist from Maine. He made a very elegant picture of a moose for me, in colored chalk, which he called, "A Moose from Maine."

The trip back took us five days compared to 7 weeks going over. The Statute of Liberty welcomed us back with open arms. There's something about the Statue of Liberty that makes you feel at home. Europe with all of it's grandeur, and antiquated history, lacks the very thing that has made America great. America is great because our forefathers sacrificed their lives for the sake of freedom.

From New York Grand Central Station I was sent to Camp Grant in Illinois to be discharged from the Army on October 24, 1945.

Grace and her family; Daytha, Alice, and Wesley were there to greet me. It was like a dream; we were three years older. The girls had changed the most, from pigtails to two beautiful young ladies. Wesley informed me he had a big American star in the window all the time I was gone. Grace had aged gracefully, a few gray hairs. They had many questions about the war and especially about Cina. When is she coming?

I spent some time in Minnesota with family and with my good friend Ellis Mooney in Sheboygan, Wisconsin. Then it was back to work in the bakery, it was time to give Grace a rest.

Cina and I kept letters flying back and forth across the ocean. It was a time I could express my love for her in writing. Separation makes the emotions run deep; for me it made me realize how much I really loved her. The time went fast but at times very slowly, especially when you are waiting for someone.

In one of her letters Cina informed me she was pregnant and it caused a lot of excitement and concern on my part. She was doctoring with an American doctor connected with the Red Cross. Complications started after a few months but the doctor insisted nothing was wrong, nothing to worry about. The hemorrhaging didn't stop and Cina's mother decided it was time to see another doctor. Pastor Vinay, the pastor that married us, knew of a Jewish doctor that he had befriended during the war and he asked him to examine Cina. After a brief examination, he found Cina was in serious condition and had to be taken to the hospital. After a thorough examination he discovered the fetus was dead and the womb had to be scraped. The hospital was still short on supplies, no anesthetics, painkillers, or clean sheets. I still shudder when I think of the ordeal Cina went through. The pregnancy was far enough along to determine it was a boy. We had decided to call our first baby boy "Richard." After a short stay in the hospital Cina was well enough to go home and slowly recovered her strength. The doctor reassured her she would be able to have many children.

Cina's father experienced the pain of saying good-bye to his only daughter, who had never been away from home before. Being the only girl in the family, Cina was his pride and joy. Now she was going to a foreign country 7,000 miles away. Sorrow and happiness are strange companions, but that is life. He was happy for Cina because she was happy; sad, for now she belonged to another and was leaving her native land. Like most Italian men, he took pride in his heritage. He taught her well. She had great love for family, music, art, and country. Cina's mother was determined and was confident she would come to America but her father was sure he would never see his lovely daughter again. He was a very sensitive man and his feelings ran deep. The best way he could express his emotions was by singing, for he had a beautiful mellow baritone voice. He sang an aria from Verdi's opera, "La Traviata" when Alfredo's Father sings to his son. *"When you leave I will suffer from your absences. It will be lonely without you. No more joy in the home,"* a very emotional song. This was very hard on Cina because she cared very much for her father. He never questioned the sincerity of Cina's love for me, while others said she sold her soul for American bread. Cina's father was the first to denounce such accusations. Some of the priests said she was making a terrible mistake; one priest in particular encouraged her to follow her heart and to stand for her convictions.

Cina's father had previously gone through a great sorrow. His eldest son was mysteriously killed on a hunting trip in Sardinia when he was 18 years old. Cina's father was an anti-fascist and never joined the Fascist movement and neither did his son. There was much suspicion about his son's death and the authorities would not investigate. Nothing was proven but always doubt lingered.

After seven months, the Red Cross notified Cina there would be room for her on a ship departing from Naples. Cina had never been to Naples before and her mother decided to accompany her. The boat was delayed and Cina and her mother were put up in an Army barracks with poor accommodations. After three days, they were notified there would be no room on the ship, they returned to Florence.

Later she found out her name was on the list but a Red Cross worker had been bribed to put someone else in her place. When the Army found out about it, they took complete charge. In two weeks Cina was notified and they reassured her there would be room.

The ship did not weather the stormy Atlantic Ocean with much grace. Conditions were very crude. The food was lousy or tasted that way because she suffered from seasickness. Most of the time, when possible, Cina stayed on the upper deck eating cheese and crackers that a sympathetic cook had given her.

Finally I received word from the Red Cross that Cina would be arriving in New York City on the steamship, "Algonquin" on April 15, 1946. They arrived in New York Harbor a day ahead of schedule and rules prevented them from disembarking but many of the passengers were sick, and the Chaplain on the boat persuaded the officers to let them disembark a day early. I was not notified of the changed schedule.

Speeding eastward on the Pacific-Atlantic Railroad halfway between Chicago and New York, I noticed in the New York Times my wife's boat had arrived a day early according to my schedule. I sent a telegram to the Red Cross stating I would be there that evening. In the meantime the Red

Cross had put her on a train for Chicago. When I arrived in New York they informed me my telegram arrived too late.

Dashing to the travel agency, next to the Grand Central Station, I purchased airfare back to Chicago and the plane would arrive before the train. I couldn't believe this was happening.

Nervously waiting for the limousine to take me to the airport, I heard a woman's voice over the loud speaker stating, "We are trying to locate Mr. Ernest Hedges. Please go to the Grand Central Station, your wife is waiting for you." I had purchased the last ticket to Chicago on that particular flight. There were passengers on stand-by. The ticket agent readily accepted my cancellation. Dashing through that huge door to the station I saw many people going in all directions.

There were other war brides; they had been roped off at the far end of the station waiting for their husbands to pick them up. There was a huge sign that read, "WAR BRIDES."

Racing to the terminal, relieved Cina was not on the train headed for Chicago, I was eager to find the love of my life. Concerned passengers were franticly looking at schedules trying to find their way through the crowd. I almost stumbled over a small child as I was straining my neck to see if I could see Cina. Suddenly I heard Cina's voice above the noise of the crowd calling my name, "Earnest." She never called me "Ernie," it was always "Earnest." There she was, we ran to each other and embraced with tears of joy. At last I had her in my arms. A news reporter looking for some news took our picture, a happy reunion, and said the picture would be in the morning paper. We vowed we would never be separated again. The waiting was over. An alert Red Cross worker had received my telegram and without telling any one, went himself and took Cina off the train just as it was departing, a divine intervention! Cina was the only "War Bride" left waiting and the Red Cross worker treated her to a "spaghetti" dinner and reassured her that her husband was on his way, which she very much appreciated. Cina looked as beautiful as ever. It was getting late and we stayed that night at the Hotel Commodore, right next to the Grand Central.

The following morning we took the train to New Jersey to see my old army friend Ernie Munseni. He was an Italian and his mother had prepared the works for us, homemade pasta, and she had made homemade cheeses strung all around the kitchen stove. What a feast! Cina felt right at home. Ernie was engaged and promised to stop and see us on their honeymoon.

From there we went to Baltimore to see Mrs. Rhodes, the woman who befriended me in Fort Meade and faithfully wrote to me and had insisted we stop to see her because she wanted to meet my new wife. She fell completely in love with Cina. She took us shopping. Finally we exchanged our brass rings for gold ones. After shopping for dresses and such, Mrs. Rhodes treated us to a Chinese dinner. From Baltimore we went to Washington D. C. I thought Cina would be delighted to see the nations' capital, instead she was thrilled to see black babies and squirrels; something they didn't have in Florence. They had plenty of statues and famous buildings.

From D. C. we flew to Chicago. This was Cina's first airplane ride. Was she excited? Not really. She slept most of the time. I can't blame her. After so much traveling, sleep was finally catching up to her. The worst of our travels was still to come. Chicago to Cambridge turned out to be a nightmare, six long hours on a bus.

How can you compare Cambridge, Wisconsin with Florence, Italy? Cambridge is a small town with one main street, a famous bakery, (of course), one telephone operator, one barbershop, one bank, Marden's Restaurant, Simonson Garage, and Prescott Furniture store. It also has a Presbyterian Church, one Lutheran Church, and the oldest Scandinavian Methodist Church in the world. What's so great about Florence? Michelangelo, Dante, great composers, and artists lived there. People go to Florence to finish their education. The Ponte Vecchio, famous paintings, great singers, and inspiring music all play a part of the history of

Florence. The great preacher, Savonarola was hanged there and then they burnt his body.

It was a colossal change for Cina, but she loved every second of it. It amazed her to see mailboxes without padlocks, homes with a yard of green grass, instead of apartments.

We stayed with Grace for a few months until we built a place of our own. That spring a robin had built its nest on the windowsill of our bedroom with 4 blue eggs that hatched in 4 baby robins. The bird was trying to tell us we would have 4 babies in our nest, which came true.

We bought a lot and built a double garage with the intention of building a house later. We fixed the double garage with 4 rooms, a kitchen, dining room, bedroom, and a bath. Instead of a door in the front, we put windows.

Cina learned to speak and understand English in no time; however, sometimes she would ask for peanuts butter. The first thing Cina wanted to do was to get her citizenship papers. She went to school and studied and passed with flying colors. It was a happy day for her when she became an American citizen.

Cina loved the Norwegian people. Cambridge was definitely a Norwegian town. It wasn't long until she had many friends, but one thing troubled her. She still wasn't pregnant. Her dream was to become a mother.

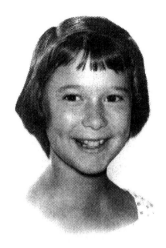

Dorothy Jean

Jane Carol

David Ernest

Jonathan Craig

Ernest, Dorothy, Cina 1947

Ernest, Cina, Jane, Dorothy 1949

Dorothy, Ernest, Guido, Cina, Tais and Jane

David, Jane, Ernest, Dorothy, Jonathan, Cina, and Tais
Madison 1960

Our first home
Cambridge, Wisconsin 1946

The double garage

Chapter 11

Two Sisters

Finally Cina became pregnant and she was happy. Our first born was a great experience. We acted like pros. Very calmly we timed the intervals of the labor pains four o'clock in the morning! Everything was happening on schedule, just as the doctor predicted. I called the doctor and we were on our way to the hospital in Fort Atkinson. The next morning at 11:00 A. M. May 21, 1947 our baby was born. She had big dark eyes and brown wavy hair. Now the pain was gone for Cina and her face had a heavenly glow.

Her dream came true. Cina was now a mother. We named our baby, Dorothy Jean. Cina's first meal in the hospital was quite shocking.... sauerkraut for an Italian girl! We had no bathinette so I gave the baby a bath on the ironing board. She was not fragile, very sturdy but not fat. Of course all fathers think their babies are the cutest but I could say it and mean it! The editor of the local Cambridge newspaper had an announcement that Ernie Hedges became the proud parent of a baby girl. If you don't believe it look at his vest. All of the buttons are gone! Dorothy Jean became everybody's sweetheart.

Our next great experience came on April 1st, 1949 when our second baby girl was born. We played the waiting game. I went home. The next day when I met the nurse, she said she had exciting news for me. "Your wife just had twins!" What a shock! "April Fool," she said with glee. It was the first of April. There was more waiting. I went downtown and bought a new suit and when I returned our baby was born.

We named her Jane Carol. Jane loved basketball. We took her to the high school games and whenever she had the chance, she would run out on the court sucking her thumb. What a cheerleader!

When Jane was a year and a half she had a fever that wouldn't go away. We took her to the hospital and after several days, the doctor called us to his office and informed us she had leukemia and probably only had three months to live. We were in shock but we finally resigned her to God's care knowing whatever the outcome, we could face tomorrow. The doctor advised us to take her to the Madison General Hospital for a second opinion. After seven doctors examined her, their conclusion was that she was cutting teeth. Did the hospital in Fort Atkinson make a mistake or was she healed? Either way we thanked the Lord and with thankful hearts we took her home and she was fine. The fever was gone.

Shortly after moving into our four room double garage we had some unexpected company. It was five o'clock in the morning when we heard someone knocking on our front door. There stood two men, one was a little taller than the other and they were definitely Italians, no doubt about that. "Hi, are you Ernie Hedges?" the shorter one asked. I assured him I was when I went to bed, now I was half awake. He put out his hand and said, "I am Lou and this is my brother Phil." This was our introduction to the Palermo Brothers. They were two Italian boys who were dedicated to singing gospel songs. They sang in churches and were active in "Youth For Christ." They made it their mission to look up all the Italian "War Brides." They said most of the "War Brides" they contacted had divorced their husbands and returned to Italy. Our marriage was the exception. Cina enjoyed meeting them and they always stopped to see us when they went through Madison. One night after a "Youth For Christ" meeting in Madison we went to a restaurant for a snack. There was a large group of young people on the street and Lou got his guitar out and asked if they would like to hear some "rock" music. The answer was in the affirmative. He sang *"Rock of Ages, Cleft for Me."* Lou was a comedian and was good at the guitar. He kept their attention and gave them a gospel concert.

Now that Cina was an American citizen she could call her parents to this country. We wanted them to wait and come after we built a house, but Cina's mother insisted to come right away. Against our better judgment we sent for them; we wanted them to wait until later. They came by boat to New York City and flew to Madison, Wisconsin. Andrea and Guido, the two brothers could not come with them according to immigration laws, only parents could come. After they were in this country, they could request unmarried children. The boys stayed with their uncle.

Cina and I were going out the door headed for Madison Airport to pick up Cina's parents when I tarried behind. I stood by Jane's crib. She was only six months old and I thought to myself; "what a beautiful and healthy baby." I was so impressed I knew that picture would always be forever stamped in my memory.

Six months after Cina's parents came; they requested permission for the boys, Andrea and Guido, to come to this country. I went to New York City and met them. At this time they couldn't speak much English, but it was good to be together again. It wasn't easy for them in school at first, but in no time they were speaking the language fluently. Andrea was 16 and Guido was going on 10.

How we managed in our small house, I will never know, but we did. Cina's mother complained and complained, but she wanted to come even though she had to sleep in a tent. Now was her chance. Even with her complaining we loved her very much.

It soon became evident the bakery wasn't large enough to support two families. Grace had good help and when I had the chance to buy a bakery twenty miles away in Madison, on Atwood Avenue, I did with a built-in clientele. We sold our double garage home to an elderly woman we knew and bought a house in Madison on Walter Street, Number 37. Ruth and Tryg Haagensen lived next door and they became our beloved neighbors.

After moving to Madison, Cina's parents and her brothers moved into an apartment of their own. Cina's mother found work as a seamstress.

The bakery on Atwood Avenue had an apartment on the second floor. A man and his wife lived there. I could see them come and go. One day a police officer came in the store and asked if so and so (I have forgotten his name) lived upstairs. I replied that he did. The officer told me they just found his body in a ditch on the edge of town and that he had been dead for several days. I looked surprised and almost laughed in his face. "It is impossible," I said, "I just saw him go upstairs a few minutes ago." The policeman looked surprised now. The body they found had identification of the man living upstairs. I called him on the phone and asked him to come down. The man that was supposed to be dead came slowly down the stairs very much alive. He was questioned by the police and told them he had lost his billfold several weeks ago with all of his credit cards, identification, and some cash. I never learned whom the man was that they found in the ditch.

Chapter 12

Two Brothers

It wasn't long until we moved the bakery to a larger building on North Street. It was at this time our son David was born in 1952. Ruth-Ann Hendrickson was working for us. I called her and left the store, we passed each other on the street. She was rushing to the bakery and I was dashing home to take Cina to the hospital. After having two girls it was nice to have a boy— just what we ordered. My brother Bob (Lewis) was in Madison at the time David was born. He predicted he would be a football player because he had such a big chest. Bob took a liking to Jane Carol and wanted to adopt her. He had one son.

A short time after David was born, I had a funny experience on North Street. One Saturday afternoon the police came rushing into the bakery to question me. They wanted to know where I was at 12:00 A. M. that morning. A jewelry store downtown had been robbed and a woman said that the robber looked like the baker on North Street. Poor guy! No, it wasn't me. I had witnesses to prove I was making bread.

After three years at North Street, the owner of the building wanted it for his own use. I couldn't find a good location for the bakery and I had a chance to work for Vim Bakery, I sold the equipment, instead of moving the bakery. Vim Bakery was on State Street between the Capitol and the University of Wisconsin.

Cina's father was getting lonesome for Florence and we were planning a trip for him back to Italy when he became ill with some kind of a bone disease in his leg. Later he developed pneumonia. He died when David was 6 months old. I regretted I couldn't do more for him. I respected him very much. He had class. He read the book of Proverbs and lived by it, a very kind and lovable person whom we loved very much.

Some things I remember about David's childhood. While playing, he hummed. His mother always knew where he was. He was strictly a diplomat. He would say, "Dad do you want me to have the black or red boots?" One time when Cina was shopping with David, who was 4 years old, he disappeared and couldn't be found. Cina was shopping at Montgomery Wards that was about four blocks from the Vim bakery. Through heavy traffic David found his way to the bakery and proudly said that every car missed him. In playing ball it was my fault if he didn't hit the ball. He would say, "Dad, you missed the bat again." One school project he had was to plant pumpkin seeds. That fall our back yard was full of pumpkins. We had to buy goat's milk at the goat farm because David was allergic to cow's milk.

I worked for the Vim Bakery for a couple of years then I took a civil service test and started working for the Post Office in 1956.

David's favorite program was "Zorro." Jonathan was born on Zorro night. I was working in the Post Office and Tryg, our neighbor, took Cina to the hospital. Two girls and two boys made four, just as the robin predicted. Jonathan was born August 1st on our 13th wedding anniver-sary, 1958. Jonathan was a happy baby, a real comedian and always made people laugh. He could talk at an early age, no baby talk for him. More about Jonathan later.

I usually lived a very peaceful life, but one night as I was on my way to the church for a special occasion, two thugs jumped in front of my car forcing me to stop. It happened so fast I didn't realize what was going on. They grabbed me and started to beat me up. The only thing I could think of was the $200 I had in my pocket. Very seldom do I carry so much cash (in fact, I very seldom had that much money.) That particular night our Pastor, Vernon Schutz and his wife Marge, took Cina and the family to the church and I was to meet them there. I was punched in the face several times and my nose started to bleed. My hair was a mess (nothing unusual). Suddenly a police car went by. He didn't see me. He didn't stop, but it did scare the thugs and they disappeared into thin air. I could feel my face swelling. One eye was swollen shut; otherwise I was in good shape. What was their motive? Was it something from the bakery they didn't like, or did they intend to rob me? I never knew. It was getting late and I hurried to the church. My plan was to slip in the back door and clean up before anybody saw me. As I entered, Marge saw me. "Ernie! What happened to you?" she asked, not believing what she saw. "Nothing," I replied, "Don't tell Cina until I clean up." After washing up I was sure I looked better than I felt.

We began to think about moving to Florida. Cina's hay fever was get-ting worse especially in the month of August. We had ordered some veg-etables from Mr. Tucker in Boca Raton, Florida, who ran a vegetable farm. When they arrived, we had 6 feet of snow piled up in our driveway. We were convinced about moving to Florida!

The 14 years we lived in Madison we enjoyed belonging to the Grace Bible Church. We cherished many memories: Laura's chicken-pot-pie—she could feed 25 or more people with a moment's notice. Gil and Ester

Nagel had an unlimited amount of hospitality. Horace Garlick was always ready with a tape recorder and a sound system. Irene and Russ Brew were always ready to help and teach. Mabel Landphier was faithful in playing the organ. Ted was a handy man for most anything; Tammingma's, Brandsma's, Don Welford, and Ed Blair were among the faithful. Dick and Phyllis Meier, were a benevolent department in themselves, always ready to help those in need. Cal and Jan Meier, Bob and Thelma Harper and of course the Beaumonts and many more we remember with fondness.

Chapter 13

First Trip To Florida

Our first trip to Florida in 1958 was in our Studebaker, the last of its kind. Studebaker went out of business in the early 60's. As we entered Florida at Fernandina Beach, we were really thirsty and when we saw a water fountain we made a dash for it. I think it was supposed to be water but it tasted like rotten eggs. It was dreadful. Is this the kind of water they have in Florida? Sulfur? It was from a deep well which contained sulfur. I never heard of it before. We were very thirsty and we had to find some good water. There was a store on the other side of the park. At least we could buy some 7-Up. In the store there were two water fountains with signs over each. One said, "White" and the other said, "Colored." David said," I want the colored water." It was our first encounter with the racial problem in the South. How could we explain this to our children? We didn't understand it ourselves. At least the water was cold and very good, not like the water in the park.

For our children, it was their first view of the Atlantic Ocean. They couldn't wait to jump in and get their feet wet. A childhood dream had come true. The huge body of water was all they had dreamed it to be. The only complaint was that it was a little salty.

We were on schedule. Another two hours we would be in Tomoka State Park, near Ormond Beach, where we camped for the night. We put up our tent and made hamburgers with all the trimmings. Since this was a State Park we thought it would be safe to leave our cooking utensils on the table. We put the bread and some cookies securely in a metal box. The next morning to our surprise everything on the table was gone. We looked around and it didn't take long to figure out what had happened. The raccoons had invaded our camp and carried the pot and pans into a near by woods. Those little animals had managed to open the box of cookies and ate them all up. We soon learned of their playful tricks.

The next morning we headed for Melbourne to find Dewy and Marian Mann. We had heard about them and the Bible class they had started. They lived in Palm Bay, a town next to Melbourne. We found them to be cordial and hospitable. Since we had a large family we camped in their back yard. After spending a couple days with the Mann's, it was time to press on to Boca Raton where Mr. Tucker had a vegetable farm. There was a possibility to find work with Mr. Tucker as he said he wanted a baker in his enterprise he was starting.

After many inquiries, we found Mr. Tucker's place. It was a well-kept farm with a large beautiful house. Mr. Tucker came out to greet us. The beautiful house and the well-kept surroundings didn't match the man we saw before us. Here was a man in his forties or fifties, with a prune like face wildly chewing peanuts, with nothing on but a pair of shorts. I introduced myself. He didn't seem impressed. Didn't he know who I was? He had encouraged me to come down. We were anxious to see inside the beautiful house. We thought we would have a nice bed to sleep in. Mrs. Tucker now came out to see us. She seemed to be quite hospitable. We exchanged some small talk while Mr. Tucker kept eating peanuts. It was getting late and since we were not invited inside I asked if we could put our tent up in their yard. "Absolutely Not!" Mr. Tucker said between peanuts. "It just wouldn't look good. It would cheapen the looks of our house." Mrs. Tucker was a real humanitarian. "After all," she said to her husband, "they are of the human element. Couldn't they camp way down in the field? Nobody would notice." They decided to let us camp in the cabbage patch. We drove down as far as we could. There was a small building in the field that had showers and toilet facilities. At least we could take showers and have use of the bathroom, but Mr. Tucker put a stop to that kind of thinking. He locked the door and said we couldn't use it. Instead he handed me a shovel. With shovel in hand I asked if the family knew what that meant. David sizing up the situation spoke up. "Well Dad, I'll be the first to use it."

It was unbelievable! Here we were in beautiful Florida, camping in a cabbage patch. We were dumbfounded! Our hopes were way down. This certainly was not the man I wanted to work for. At least they recognized us as a part of the human race and not somebody from Mars!

It was getting dark and in silence we ate the sandwiches Mrs. Mann had fixed for us. We got some water from a garden hose for drinking. The vote was unanimous. We would get up early in the morning and leave before sunrise. Very slowly we pulled passed the house. We didn't want the Tuckers to hear us. What a relief to be on the highway. We didn't look back. We arrived in Palm Bay, too late for church, but just in time for a potluck dinner. (Of course, they invited us)

After spending some time in Melbourne and Palm Bay, we went back to Camp Tomoka and spent a lot of time at Ormand Beach. We rented a cabana and lived on the beach the rest of our vacation. The girls, Dorothy and Jane, got their share of the sun while the boys, David and Jonathan, had fun riding the waves. Cina and I walked up and down the beach. Vacation over, we headed north, we knew we were back in Wisconsin. A chill went down my back. It was the last of August but it was cool and didn't warm up until spring.

Chapter 14

Second Trip To Florida

Five years went by before our second trip to Florida. This time we had a Fire-Chief Pontiac. Instead of camping, we rented a cabin on the Indian River in Grant, Florida.

The plumbing wasn't so good in the cabin. Dorothy was taking a shower and the handle on the hot water faucet came off. She couldn't turn the steaming hot water off and was trapped in the corner of the shower. Her screaming and hollering brought me to the scene in a hurry. "Do something Dad," she cried. With a pair of pliers I very bravely reached in and turned the hot water off. She had an unexpected steam bath, so did I.

While the family spent time on the beach, I looked the town over to buy a house. One more day before we were to return to Madison and I hadn't found a house to buy. I had one more house to check out, a house on Espanola Way. This turned out to be the best deal yet. I could assume the G. I. Mortgage at 4% interest with $1000 down. Cina agreed it was a good deal. We bought the house and had it rented. The 4% mortgage sort of reveals my age. It was August 1963.

Chapter 15

Postal Clerk Back To Baking

Working in the post office was not for me. I learned every street on the west and east side of Madison as well as the downtown area. It was a great exercise for my memory. I loved that part of it, but sitting at a desk sorting mail into the different pigeonholes was murder for my back and neck. The pain in my neck was getting me down but fortunately I was put on registered mail and that gave me freedom to walk around. I even carried a gun and would have to take registered mail personally to the train and hand it to the clerk in charge. Sometimes it would involve large sums of money.

I witnessed the rise and fall of the postal system. The first year working in the Madison post office the workers took pride in their work. Speed and efficiency were in. Abraham Lincoln said *"You cannot strengthen the weak by weakening the strong."* In other words, "you cannot speed up the slow by slowing down the fast." The new system of measuring the mail did exactly that. The ones I admired for their speed slowed down to be average. Speed was out, average was in.

We had tons of junk mail, most of it at the cost of the taxpayers. One time we discovered some of the so-called "junk mail" was communistic propaganda. Enough of the workers complained and the Postmaster had it removed. I never knew what happened to it. There were two card-carrying communists working in the post office that I knew.

I was making bread for home use at Triggs' old Bakery on Johnson Street. Triggs had started a new bakery on the East Side Shopping Center. The old bakery was for sale. One time Mr. Triggs asked me how much would I offer him for the bakery. In a very kidding way I said I wouldn't give him over $300. "Sold," he said before I had the chance to catch my breath. Was it a deal? He thought it was and come to think about it I thought so too. The oven was old but in good condition. The mixer made a lot of noise but it worked. I couldn't go wrong on $300. I got busy and planned my next move. Eight hours in the post office, eight hours in the bakery, and eight hours to sleep. I could manage. I hired Mrs. Sullivan to wait on customers. I baked at night and worked in the post office in the daytime. There had been a bakery at this location on Johnson Street for 100 years. It was well known. In no time business was great. I sold out each day and sold more each day.

One evening I came to the store and Mrs. Sullivan was kneeling on the floor mumbling some words I couldn't understand. My first thought was that she was speaking in tongues. I knew she went to the Lutheran Church, but I didn't think they spoke in tongues. I came a little closer to her and discovered she was having a heart attack. Mrs. Sullivan was trying to tell me to call a friend of hers. She gave me a scare but in a few days she was back to work. She was a very faithful and a wonderful friend.

Chapter 16

Florida Here We Come

We definitely decided to move to Florida. Why not move when the children are young? Why wait until we retire to enjoy Florida. After our first trip to Florida, we put our house up for sale. Our second trip, we bought a house on Espanola Way in Melbourne and rented it until we were ready to move. Our house in Madison had been listed for sale for five years and nobody was interested. Not one call. We decided to rent it and move to Florida because Cina's hay fever was getting worse. What to do with the bakery? That was the question.

One day a young baker came in the shop and asked if I wanted to sell the bakery. I said I would if the price was right, so I asked him to make me an offer. Business was good that day and the store was full of customers.

Without hesitation he made an offer of $3,500. I didn't have to do much thinking; I paid $300 for it and we wanted to move to Florida. I was told to buy low and sell high, now was my chance. Without showing too much emotion I agreed. He quickly wrote a check for the amount and now he was the owner of a going business with a built-in-clientele. He was happy and I was happy.

Believe it or not, before the day was over my real estate agent, Paul Stewart, called and said he had sold our house and received cash, all I had to do was to sign the papers and pick up the check. The Lord works in mysterious ways His wonders to perform. Five years without an offer for the house and now both the house and the bakery sold the same day for cash! The door was opened now for our move to Florida.

I was without a job and because the house was sold, we had to be out in 30 days. Our renter in Florida was given 2 weeks notice. I decided to go to Florida to look for employment and also to get the house in shape. I really didn't want to go back in the bakery business. I was fortunate to get a tremendous low bus fare to Melbourne, Florida—$51 round trip. After arriving in Melbourne, I rented a car. In Madison I was an Amway distributor, on the side, and decided to do the same in Melbourne until I discovered there were 10 distributors in a small area. I decided the competition would to too great for a full time business. I checked with the post office; they weren't hiring at the present, perhaps in another year or two. The Dunkin Donut Shop needed help; I decided to try it just to see if I would like it. It wasn't what I wanted. There was a restaurant for sale on U. S. Highway 1 and Babcock Street, which would make a combination restaurant and bakery. It was a possibility. The Melbourne Shopping Center had just opened. Next door to Publix's Grocery was Mather's Bakery and Mr. Mathers wanted to sell. This was before Publix took over the bakery. This was an opportunity, but I still kept looking.

I had rented a room on Strawbridge Avenue. One morning the woman of the house showed me the Melbourne newspaper. A bakery was for sale on New Haven Avenue. She thought I would be interested. I checked it out. Coleman's Bakery, 817 East New Haven Avenue in downtown Melbourne was for sale…just my size. Mr. Coleman had just turned 65 and was ready to retire. It was a neat bakery shop. I had the feeling this was it but didn't want to make a decision until I talked with Cina. I went back to Madison with two possibilities; the restaurant and the bakery. When I arrived back in Madison I discovered they were freezing while I was enjoying the warm July spring air of Florida. They had the furnace on full blast.

It was hard to leave our friends and the church we were attending. The following is a note we received from Grace Bible Church in Madison, Wisconsin;

Dear Friends;

There comes a time when we must say farewell, to those we hold most dear, and there is always a moment of sadness, when the time draws near. We will miss you all so very much, far more than words can tell, yet we know you'll be safe in the Savior's love, and so we wish you well.. We'll miss the lovely voice that sang our Savior's praises too. Remember us always in your prayers, as we'll remember you.

Friends from GBC

It was time to pack. We rented a large U-Haul truck. Rollin Wilson was our Pastor at the time and he took charge of loading. To my amazement he packed things so tight we had room to spare, he really was an expert at loading. In fact, he was so good that he put 4 small coaster-legs to Jane's bed in a lunch bucket; we didn't find them until 2 years later. By evening everything was packed, ready to take off early the next morning.

Ruth and Tryg, our next-door neighbors, had invited all of the kids of the neighborhood in for hamburgers. As I remember they were delicious. We had fun but down deep in our hearts we were sad to be leaving such wonderful friends. That night we had a fierce windstorm. In front of the bay window we had a trellis covered with purple wisteria. The wind completely turned it into a twisted mess. I felt a little guilty driving away leaving things in such a clutter for the new owners. Branches from trees were scattered around the yard. I drove the truck with David in the front seat. Cina drove the Pontiac with Dorothy, Jane, Jonathan, and "Annie-Pie" our boxer, and a cat. I noticed David was fighting to keep the tears back and I didn't dare say anything, unless it might reveal my emotions. Leaving such good friends is not easy to do. Silence was our companion until we were through Beloit and when we crossed the Illinois line we broke the silence and remembered the good hamburgers Ruth and Tryg had made the night before for all of the kids. David was happy now and began talking about the ocean and the big waves. He had fallen in love with Florida in our two trips there and was looking forward to swimming and fishing and, of course, surfing.

It wasn't easy to find a motel we could stay in with 4 kids, a dog, and a cat. We slept two nights in motels and the third night we stayed with my niece, Milly and her husband Dr. John Beggs. They lived in Lake City, Florida.

The next day we arrived in Melbourne about 3 o'clock in the afternoon, August 1, 1964. Dewy Mann came and helped to unload. It was Jonathan's fifth birthday and our 19th wedding anniversary. I have forgotten what we did for our anniversary, (probably nothing) but we bought Jonathan his first two-wheel bicycle.

Chapter 17

The New Bakery

When Cina saw the bakery, we decided to buy it and with no time lost we were in business, Sept.1,1964. Mr. and Mrs. Coleman worked with us for a couple of weeks. I wanted to learn the way he did things and Cina learned cake decorating from Mrs. Coleman. Before we knew it we were in full swing. The first big order came at the dedication of the new Sebastian Inlet Bridge that connected the Indian River with the Atlantic Ocean. Cina had to draw the high-rise bridge across the inlet on a large sheet cake. It turned out beautifully and it gave our bakery some free advertisement.

Our first month in business we had the excitement of a hurricane, called Cleo. It was late in the afternoon and Cina and I noticed no cars in the street and no one in sight. We decided we had better head for home. At that time there was a large fruit stand on the corner of New Haven and Babcock Street. Bunches of bananas were swinging in the wind. We thought by the next day the fruit would be scattered all over the street. To our surprise when we went to work the next morning, the bananas were still swaying in the breeze and all the fruit and vegetables were intact. During the night the eye of the hurricane broke up and didn't reorganize until it passed. Melbourne. Cleo was a major hurricane, but very little damage occurred in Melbourne. The only damage was on the beaches.

One time a lady ordered a large birthday cake and when she arrived home she discovered the one large candle she ordered was missing. She lived on the beach and didn't have time to come in and pick it up. It was impossible for me to leave the store and nobody was around that I could send. I called a taxicab and had the driver deliver the one candle. It paid off because she became a very good customer and she told her many friends about the bakery.

The next main event came when a young reporter from a local radio station "WMEL" came in the bakery. He sold us on the idea that some advertising would help our business as we were planning a grand opening. We also were changing the name of "Coleman Bakery" to "HEDGES BAKERY." The reporter's name was Karl Meier. That was our first intro-duction to the handsome young reporter who became a regular customer. Thanks to our new friend our advertising paid off and the grand opening was a huge success. Karl became a frequent visitor to our bakery and to our home. His father had died and his mother lived in Indialantic. Karl lived on his boat on the Indian River. He soon left the radio station and became a State Farm Insurance Agent. Karl started his insurance business from scratch and couldn't afford to pay much for a secretary. He asked me if I knew anybody that would be interested.

When Dorothy graduated from high school, she went to Puerto Rico for the summer as a teen missionary. At that time Dorothy had just returned from Puerto Rico and now was working as a cashier at

Montgomery Wards and she was planning on going to Grace Bible College in the fall. I thought maybe Jane would be interested even though she was taking a correspondence course in airline stewardship. Jane had just finished high school and was going to a business college. She took the secretarial job with Karl, but also continued her pursuit as an airline stewardess.

When Dorothy was a senior in high school, she was in a choral group. They were invited to give a concert in Minneapolis. At that time my two brothers Elmer and Lewis were living there. I told Dorothy to be sure and call them and say hello for me. When she returned home I asked her, "Did you call your uncles?" Dorothy replied, "I couldn't remember their last names." "Dorothy" I said in surprise, "it's the same as yours!"

At Jane's graduation from high school the ceremony was held outdoors in the football field. Just before it ended it started to rain and everybody got wet, especially Cina. By the time we reached the car the dress Cina was wearing shrunk so much it looked like a bikini. She was so embarrassed.

Chapter 18

Dorothy's Wedding

While going to Grace Bible College, Dorothy met Paul Olsen and they dated. Dorothy came home for summer vacation and started dating a baseball player who was with the Minnesota Twins. At that time the Twins had their training camp in Melbourne. Paul had different plans. He had planned on coming to Melbourne to give Dorothy an engagement ring. To his utter amazement she wasn't ready to accept it. Paul in his frustration threw the ring in some bushes. David and Jonathan retrieved the ring and told Paul he had better keep it, as he still might need it. The ballplayer, (I think his name was Figaro) wanted Dorothy to meet his folks who lived in New York. After a short trip there, she was back in

Melbourne and soon was on her way to Chicago. Before we knew it Paul and Dorothy announced their engagement and a wedding date was set.

Dorothy's desire was to be married in her home church in Madison, Wisconsin. She was working in Chicago and we had the bakery in Melbourne, Florida. Also she wanted us to make her wedding cake. That created a problem to deliver a wedding cake 1400 miles away. We would figure out a way. In the bakery business we always had unusual situations to solve. We had the practice of closing the bakery for a couple of weeks during the summer. The day before we closed, we baked a four-tier wedding cake and wrapped each layer in plastic and Reynolds wrap. The icing was prepared and put in large containers. We also had a large German chocolate sheet cake and the ingredients to make the icing.

After loading up and closing the bakery on Saturday, we started out about six o'clock in the evening. Since David just received his restricted driver's license, he drove in Florida until we crossed the Georgia state line. We drove all night and all day Sunday and arrived at Paul's parents in Chicago at midnight. Early the next morning we headed for Madison. The first thing we did was to unload the cakes into freezers in a school where Esther Nagel worked. The next Saturday morning before the wedding, we took the cake and icing to the church. Cina decorated the cake while I went to Pastor Wilson's house and made the icing for the German chocolate cake. It solved our problem and the cakes tasted oven fresh.

Paul and Dorothy were married at Grace Bible Church on Painted Post Drive in Madison, Wisconsin on June 22, 1968. It was a beautiful ceremony. Facing each other, Paul and Dorothy sang a duet, a wedding song written by Vern Stromsburg. The reception followed at the church. The ladies of the church put on a real feast. The wedding was well organized and made it very enjoyable. Everything seemed to just flow. The evening before the wedding Art Olsen, Paul's father treated all of the relative and friends to a banquet at a fancy restaurant in Madison. There was a shivery and some pranks on the newlyweds. I will let Paul write about it in his "life story."

Jane flew up for the wedding and helped us drive back. Our air conditioner went out going through Georgia and we cooked the rest of the way home.

Chapter 19

Ups and Downs

Families have their ups and downs. We had our ups and downs, but I can truly say we had mostly ups.

It was a sad day when we had to put Annie Pie (our boxer) to sleep. She was dying from heartworms. She was like one of the family. One funny incident happened when Wesley Josephson came to see us. It was raining and Wesley wanted to go for a walk. He took the big beach umbrella we had and went for a walk down the street. He visited with all of the neighbors. When he came back, it was really pouring rain. Wesley, with the beach umbrella, was walking in the middle of the street and a lone duck was following him. I wished I had a camera, as it was a funny sight.

David missed his graduation because he went surfing and forgot to come home in time. We got there too late, but we did hear his name over the loud speaker. He received his diploma the next day. He was on time for his college graduation.

One of the downs for us was when Jane decided to move out and have her own apartment. At first it gave us a guilt complex. What did we do wrong? That is usually the reaction parents have. No matter how much we wanted her to stay home, she had made up her mind. She packed her clothes in a suitcase and started walking down the street. That tore me up. I decided I could take her wherever she was going. With eyes full of tears, I got in the car and caught up with her and asked if I could take her. Jane had found a room with a little old lady who lived on Lincoln Street. She stayed there for a couple of weeks and later rented an apartment with a girlfriend. That lasted a short time and within a month she was back home again.

I must tell you of the tale of the rusty nail. When I was mowing the yard the force of the mower picked up a rusty nail and embedded it in the calf of my leg. At first I thought it was a stone or a piece of wood that hit my leg. It was bleeding and I called Cina, but she didn't hear me. I crawled to the house and put pressure on the wound and washed it off. It did stop bleeding and I forgot about it. In a couple days my leg began to swell and was becoming very painful I decided to see the doctor. The first thing he did was to take an x-ray that revealed a nail about three inches long. The doctor became very concerned. He said it was probably very infected and I would have to go to the hospital for treatment, however, he could remove the nail in his office. To his great surprise it showed no sign of infection. He couldn't understand it. A rusty nail in my leg for three days was a sure sign of blood poisoning. What the doctor didn't know and I didn't tell him was that my wife had given me a mega dose of vitamin C and A and that evidently stopped the infection.

It was a few days before Christmas when our gas stove at home exploded and Cina's left leg was severely burned. First degree burns. We had been told that aloe vera was very good for burns. Our first introduction to the aloe plant was by Dr. June, a chiropractor. One day she brought a lot of aloe to the bakery for Cina to use on her burn. Dr. June was on her way to a wedding. She was a lovely lady and very elegantly dressed. To our astonishment she smelled as though she hadn't taken a bath for weeks. Her body odor was overwhelming, we thought. Later we discovered it wasn't her, it was the aloe she had brought to us! It worked fantastically. Aloe is cooling and relieves pain. It also cleans off all of the old skin. Cina's doctor said whatever she was doing to keep it up for the burn was healing remarkably well.

Sitting at a table with her burnt leg on a chair, Cina decorated cakes and she never missed a day of work.

This is a poem Cina wrote while she was recovering from her burnt leg.

LOVERLY
All I have is a room somewhere
Breezed and warm Florida air
With one enormous bed
Oh, isn't it just Loverly.
Oh so Loverly sitting
Absolutely still
It looks like I won't budge till spring
Oh isn't it just Loverly.
Lots of Aloe for me to use
Lots of gauze, lots of ointment too
Smooth feet, smooth legs, smooth hands,
Oh, isn't it just Loverly.
But, someone's here
That you cannot see
Warm and tender as He can be
Oh, isn't it just Loverly
Loverly Loverly Loverly!!!!

When we still lived on Espanola Way, the TV was in the Florida room that was closed off by sliding glass doors. David was watching an exciting football game. During the half he decided to get some ice cream. Dashing up, and forgetting the glass door was closed, he crashed into it and broke it into thousands of pieces. He was badly cut and Cina and I took him to the emergency room. He was sewed up and fortunately he had no lasting scars.

Paul and Dorothy lived in Des Plains, a suburb of Chicago after their marriage. Dewey Mann called me one night and wanted to know if Paul would be interested in working in Palm Bay, a town next to Melbourne. Dewey was the Building Inspector in Palm Bay and was ready to retire. He wanted to train someone to take his place. He thought of Paul and gave him first choice. It didn't take much for Paul and Dorothy to make a decision. The answer was positive. They were soon on their way to Florida in 1972. Shawn was 3 years old and Shannon was one year old. Timothy was born later in Melbourne on October 5, 1975. They lived in our house on Espanola Way and we moved in the apartment over the bakery. Only Jonathan was with us. David was going to college in Gainesville.

Holidays at the bakery we worked like a team, the whole family was involved. Each one had a particular job to do. Jane was an expert at folding bakery boxes. Karl helped to put up orders and delivered them. Dorothy waited on customers and Paul helped mix dough and make fillings for pies or whatever had to be done. David and Jonathan worked at the sink washing pots and pans; all the time wishing they were surfing. We had many specialties; sprouted wheat, Italian, rye, and salt rising breads. German chocolate cakes were popular and also frozen orange cakes. For pies it was pumpkin, pecan, apple mincemeat, and lemon. Danish rolls and donuts were favorites for morning coffee breaks. Decorated cakes were the major part of our business; that was Cina's department and her fabulous artistic ability added to the prestige of the bakery.

New Year's Day 1973 I had my first bout with dizziness. I rolled out of bed and my head began to spin. It lasted only a few minutes. Usually I went to work at 4 o'clock in the morning and at 6 o'clock Mrs. Ray came in and made coffee and I would have a glazed donut. It soon dawned on me after eating a glazed donut I became very nauseated and dizzy. No more donuts for me. It helped some but I still had dizzy spells off and on. I talked to a woman in the Health Food Store and she told me exactly what I had. It was an infection in the inner ear, the labyrinth. The name for it is Meniere Syndrome. She recommended the "B" complex vitamin and to refrain from eating sweets and fried foods. I did what she said, but I still went to see a doctor.

My family doctor said he couldn't do anything for me and recommended a specialist who put me on chelation treatments. After 6 months of treatments, we went to visit my niece and her husband, Milly and Dr. John Beggs. While there I had the worst attack of dizziness yet. It lasted several days. My head started to spin, I was on the floor but felt like I was falling through space, never hitting bottom. Dr. Beggs was with the Veterans Hospital in Lake City, Florida, but recommended the Veterans Hospital in Gainesville, they had specialists for the ear. He made arrangements for me to be examined.

Seven doctors examined me and all came to the same conclusion. They couldn't do anything for me. I had Meniere Syndrome and there was no known cure. The best they could do was to furnish me with Mclezine. They assured me it was not a harmful drug. I did lose hearing in my right ear. I didn't see much improvement until I went to a doctor recommended to me by a customer that had the same problem. I was so dizzy I had to be wheeled in to see the doctor. The doctor gave me a mega shot of vitamin "B-12." By the time I arrived home I was feeling fine. After several shots, I was much better. I have learned to control it by taking long walks, breathing deeply, and taking vitamin B-12. I haven't had a sign of dizziness for the last ten years.

Chapter 20

Selene and David

Karl and Jane were dating, but nothing serious. Jane had one month left on her correspondence course she was taking to become an airline hostess. She had to go in person to Chicago for an on-the-job training. Everything was ready, suitcase packed, ready to leave. A few days before she was to leave, Karl surprised her by giving her an engagement ring. So much for on-the-job training and my hopes of getting free airfare passes.

Jane and Karl were married at the Grace Bible Church in Palm Bay, Florida on March 20, 1970. By this time Karl had sold his boat that he was living on and had bought a house in Port Malabar. Karl and Jane lived there when Selene and David were born. Selene was born Feb. 17,1971 and David was born Feb. 24,1972. Many times Jane would go shopping and leave Selene with us at the bakery. We put her on the table in her little basket. She was good as pie! (Hedges Pie) Maybe a little taste of icing now and then helped. What can I say about Selene and David? They were lovable, adorable, mischievous, cute, active, inquisitive, creative, and sensitive. Remember the Kattsenjammer Kids? That was Selene and David. One time Jane went shopping and left the kids home with Karl. On returning she discovered all of the beautiful Christmas presents were opened and wrapping paper torn to bits by little hands. She had the privilege of wrapping all the gifts the second time. The question was, where was Karl? Who knows!

Cina and I enjoyed going on boat rides with Jane and Karl and the kids. One time we went to Jacksonville, via the James River. David Hedges was working for the Time Union Newspaper at the time. David Meier was good at playing rummy. He could always get the best of me; he was about nine years old.

Battleship was another game we played. Selene and David were active in the Awana Club in the church and Cina and I would take them. I only wished we had seat belts then! It seemed they were always where they shouldn't be. It got quite wild sometimes, especially when we picked up other kids. One time we were asked to take two little girls home. We had no idea where they lived. They kept saying, "Follow the yellow line in the road." Finally we took them to the school they attended and then they were able to tell what yellow line to follow to their house.

Karl's grandmother, Mabel, had died a few years before and now his mother Alma was dying from cancer. She wanted to do something nice for Karl and Jane so she took them on a trip to Hawaii. On the way home she became ill and when they arrived in Melbourne she was taken directly to the hospital. She died a few days afterwards

Chapter 21

Michigan Street

When I turned 65, we planned on selling the bakery. I could only work part time and Cina's wrists were getting weak from so much decorating. With some mutual funds I was able to buy an acre of land in West Melbourne for $5,000. The same lots are going for $35,000 now. We built our house on Michigan Street (an A Frame) and moved in February 14, 1977 (Valentine's Day). In the morning Cina and I went to work as usual and Paul, Karl and men from the church did the moving. In the evening when we went to the house, everything was in place and since it was Valentine's Day we took our wives to Musicana, a restaurant with lots of good food and singing.

Later in the same year, 1977, our church was having a convention in Estes Park, Colorado. Paul had a van and so did Karl. We decided to take both vans and the whole family would go——all eleven of us. David was working in Jacksonville and Jon was also working, they couldn't make it. The vans were equipped with CB radios; which proved to be a blessing. It helped to keep the vans together and especially the time when Selene was left behind. It happened when we stopped at a rest area. We were well on our way when Cina suggested we call the other van to make sure we had all of the kids. Each van thought that the ones not in their van would be in the other. After calling back and forth, we discovered Selene was missing. She was 6 years old at the time. We went back to the rest area. There were some anxious moments and Selene was somewhat shaken up. One other time we couldn't find Selene. This time she was in the rest room and the door was too hard for her to open.

Going through Kansas we stopped to see my brother Wilbur and his wife Ann, also Betty Ann and Quinten, her husband. The farm had been sold and Wilbur moved to Courtland. The house and the barn on the farm were moved to a near by town. We had a wonderful time and I still remember the good food.

We enjoyed the convention and Estes Park, also The Tetons, Old Faithful, Yellowstone National Park, and Mount Rushmore. Coming home through St. Louis we had trouble finding a place to stay. Every motel was filled. We drove late into the night before we found a room. All eleven of us shared it. The whole trip was quite an experience.

Our A-Frame house
2701 Michigan St
West Melbourne, Florida

Chapter 22

Good Friends

In 1978 we sold the bakery. I always referred to the bakery as my "Salt Mine," but I must confess I enjoyed the work. It was like my second home. The customers seemed like family and some wonderful and lasting friendships were made. Our greatest concern was to use the best ingredients, such as unbleached white flour, whole-wheat flour, raw sugar, honey, and vegetable oil. Nutrition was our priority. All recipes were made from scratch, no prepared mixes or preservatives. It truly was home style baking.

Cathy was a good friend and customer who operated a health shop called "Fruit Tree" on the beach. She used our 100% sprouted whole wheat bread for sandwiches and served our carrot cake with cream cheese icing. Bob Forrester was another friendly person that kept our refrigeration in good running condition.

Later Bob and Cathy were married. The young people at that time were very health conscious and gave us a lot of business for sprouted whole wheat bread and I made yogurt by the gallon. The top of the oven proved to be an ideal place to make yogurt, just the right temperature. Another good friend was John Biddulph who was a student at Florida Institute of Technology. After graduation he worked in Hawaii for several years. He was a world traveler. When he was in Turkey he climbed Mount Ararat in search of Noah's Ark. He could write a book on his travels.

One time he came to our home and showed me a Bible and asked me if I recognized it. I said, "I never saw it before." "Funny," he said, "you gave it to me 15 years ago." Sure enough my name was in it. We were having a "Christ Formed In You" seminar in our church and I called John and asked if he would care to go. He said, "Sure, can I bring my girl friend?" They came and never missed a night. Now they are married and have three sons. Also they are active in Christian work. John knew Cathy and Bob Forrester and invited them to church. Now they attend regularly. They invited their friends, Jim and Shirley Burnett to church. Now they come and are interested in Bible study. It reminds me of a song we sing, "Pass It On." It just takes a spark to start a fire…

One Thanksgiving day we were invited to a mission in Melbourne. We knew the director. Our good friends and neighbors from Madison were here, Ruth and Tryg Haagensen. They went with us. The mission was called "Broken Glass" as it dealt with alcoholics. One of them came to Tryg and said "God bless you." Later Tryg said it was the first time he was blessed by a bum.

Chapter 23

Unconditional Grace Love

Jane and Karl's marriage was not sailing smoothly. Cina and I made it a point not to interfere in their marriage. We failed to hear their cries for help. They were divorced in 1981. It was a time of sadness. After three years they remarried in 1984.

In 1985, my oldest sister Pearl celebrated her 90th birthday. Cina and I flew to Minneapolis and so did Dorothy and Jane. Paul, Karl, and all of their kids drove up in the van. We met them in Minneapolis and then we went to Milaca where Pearl lived. It was a family reunion. Many cousins, nieces, and nephews that I hadn't seen for many years were there. Don Bettis, Pearl's son, treated the whole gang to a delicious banquet. It was a reunion to remember. Cina and I went home with Hazel and spent some time with her. Barton Hedges, my nephew and his wife Dale took us to Eau Claire, Wisconsin where Cina's two brothers lived, Andrea and Guido. From there we took a bus to Eunice and Kurt's. They took us to Madison to see a friend. My friend, Gil Nagel, had moved and we couldn't find his house. We had quite a time looking for it. We enjoyed being with Eunice and Kurt. Kurt had been sick and wasn't feeling well. Since we didn't find the Nagels, I called a friend near by. Eunice was anxious to get Kurt home before dark. That was the last time we saw Kurt. Two weeks later he died very suddenly. He was suffering from an infected foot that wouldn't heal.

Shortly after Pearl's birthday party, Jane and Karl were divorced again. We didn't understand, just accepted it. Karl was very much a part of the family. Jane wanted it that way. Since his grandmother and mother died, he had no immediate family. We still treat him as our son-in-law and is included in family gatherings. We try not to judge motives, rather to show forth-unconditional grace love. Not to forgive is detrimental, physically and spiritually.

Chapter 24

David's Wedding

David's wedding took place in Vero Beach, Florida in 1983. David met Merle, his wife to-be when he was working in Jacksonville for The Times Union Newspaper. Vero Beach was Merle's hometown. A short time before they were married, The Times Union was sold and the new owner's policy was to keep the young employees but not anyone over 50. David didn't want that to happen to him in later years and he made the decision to change jobs. There was an opening for a State Farm Insurance agency in Vero and soon after they were married, David and Merle built the agency to a successful insurance business.

They had a beautiful wedding with all of the trimmings. I made a four-tier wedding cake with almond filling and Cina with her expertness decorated it.

Merle loved it and that made Cina and me happy. During refreshments a pianist played to entertain. After he was through, Jonathan went to the piano and gave a great performance that surprised everyone and he received a thundering applause.

Chapter 25

Jonathan's Wedding

Jonathans' wedding! Since the world began, there has never been such an event. Maybe it was like when Adam and Eve were married. I wonder if they had a ceremony? They had no minister, no bridesmaid or best man. We know it happened in a garden and so did Jonathan and Linda's. First you have to understand Jonathan. He was allergic to neckties. To dress up was too uncomfortable. Why use a belt when a string would do? He would never win an award for the best-dressed man but what he did have was a heart as big as all outdoors. Jon would never pass by someone in need, like a woman stranded on the highway with a flat tire. He was especially good with old people. One time a bag woman came in the bakery and asked for Mr. Hedges. I assumed she meant me so I asked her what I could do for her. "I don't want you," she snapped. "I want Johnny." Later I asked Jon how he knew this lady. He said one time in a grocery store this lady had stolen some apples and was arrested. Jon happened to be there and offered to pay for the apples if they would let her go. She never forgot it.

Jon was a good storyteller. He could imitate Paul Harvey to a T. He loved to play the guitar and wrote his own songs, like the one called "Poor People Living Next to Rich People." The wedding march was played on a tape recorder. The setting was our back yard with all the family standing around in a group. We were living at 2701 Michigan Street at the time, February 1985.

Selene was dressed in a white dress looking more like the bride than the bride. I finally found a shirt for Jon. They both had blue jeans, right in style. Pastor Cal Boduestch performed the ceremony. To keep in tune with the situation he took off his coat and tie and rolled up his sleeves. Linda looked up at Jon and smiled when the preacher said "for richer or for poorer I bequeath all of my worldly goods…" I had baked a wedding cake and Cina had prepared a delicious meal. Like Pastor Tim says, "We have the liberty to be ourselves." Jon is definitely Jon.

When Joshua was two years old, Jon and Linda lived on a boat in the Indian River. One memory Cina and I will long remember; Linda had come to the house with Joshua to do the washing. Cina and I took her back to the river. Jonathan met us with his small motorboat that would take them to the larger boat. The Indian River is about two miles wide. Jon did a lot of clamming and shrimping at that time and had some large shrimp baskets on the motorboat. He put Joshua in one of them for safe-keeping. As they pulled out, we could see little Joshua with a proud look on his face in the shrimp basket. The sun was just setting and the sky was many shades of red. We watched that precious cargo fade in the distance until they reached the large boat; it was just a silhouette against the evening sky. It was a beautiful picture.

Chapter 26

One More Makes Ten

When Brooke, my son David's youngest child was born Cina and I were the proud grandparents of nine grandchildren— 4 grandsons and 5 granddaughters. THAT IS WHAT WE THOUGHT! Unknown to us we had another granddaughter. We discovered we had a granddaughter we had never seen and now was 16 years old. About 10 years ago, Jon received a letter from a 6-year-old girl stating that he was her father. Upon questioning, Jonathan said it was not true and that the mother of the child was trying to get support from him. I begged Jonathan to tell me the truth and if he weren't the father, I would believe him and I would never mention it again. Jonathan still maintained his innocence.

A guilty conscience is a terrible thing. For 16 years Jon lived under this cloud. He knew this child was his. In the meantime he married and had two beautiful children, Amy and Joshua. In spite of his many misdeeds, Jon never lost his faith in God. One time stopping at a filling station, in the rest room, he saw scribbled on the wall——

GOD IS DEAD
Signed—John
JOHN IS DEAD
Signed—GOD

No matter where he went, his mother's prayers followed him. Jonathan was stopped by a police officer for a very minor traffic violation. The officer noticed he was wanted for child support; that was enough to land him in jail.

We usually called Jonathan, Jon most of the time. Jon always carried his New Testament with him. In jail he saw an opportunity to minister to those who had no hope. Jon has the ability to communicate with people of all walks of life. He has an outstanding vocabulary. He couldn't complain that he was in jail because he knew he was reaping what he had sown.

Through many chain of events, Jon came to realize he had to make things right. He had a burning desire to find this unknown daughter. The HRS would not reveal where she lived, they only demanded child support. At this time, Jon came to us for help to locate his long lost daughter.

My task was before me. I have played the role of many things, now it was time to be a detective. I went to the library and looked through telephone books for the last ten years. The only thing I had to go by was the woman's name. I found her name and address, except for the last two years. Her name had been dropped, no longer in the telephone book. I checked with all of the surrounding towns. Nothing! We checked with the last address, it was only four blocks from where we lived. They knew of no such woman. Our next conclusion was that she had married. A trip to the courthouse revealed that she had. Now we had her address and telephone number. We were filled with apprehension. What kind of a reception would we have? It was time to find out.

Cina called and an appointment was set to meet. We were received very cordially. It was a very moving experience. Her name was new to us, "Chanda." Chanda was very quiet, calm and collected, but very much in charge. She had games to play with her newfound sister and brother. She was very happy to meet her father and was overjoyed to have a sister. Likewise, Amy was very happy to have an older sister. Chanda and Joshua look very much alike. Both are the quiet type and very talented in drawing, already, they have won awards and honors in art. Chanda's step dad was very good to her and wanted to adopt her, but Chanda knew that some day her real father would find her.

We have family gatherings and we are happy to welcome Chanda to the "Fold." She added much to our happiness.

On Chanda's 17th birthday, Dorothy and Jane had a birthday party for her. Since we had missed her first 16 birthdays, the two aunts had a special gift for each year of her life. The gift matched the age. They varied from a baby rattler to a shopping gift certificate. Chanda has become active in the youth group at church. We love her very much and are happy to have 10 grandchildren.

Chapter 27

Nonna Tais

In 1984 Tais, Cina's mother, came to live with us. Her second husband, Vito Justiliano, had died from cancer. She was 83 at the time and unable to live alone.

There are many kinds of prisoners. Some are behind bars, but the worst kinds are those who are trapped behind their boredom. My mother-in-law was such a person. She didn't knit or crochet, read or write letters. The only amusement she had was talking and that isn't much fun when you are alone. She never learned to amuse herself when she was alone. She wanted somebody doing things for her and with her. Some things you can do only alone. Happy is the person who has a hobby of some kind they can enjoy. Contentment is a virtue. Cina and I were prisoners of a different kind.

One of us had to stay home with her or take her along. Nonna Tais was a wonderful person and we enjoyed having her and we loved her very much. She grew up at the time of World War 1 and had experienced some turbulent times in her childhood.

July 1991 Tais became ill and was taken to the hospital. She was 90 years old at the time. Doctors informed us she would have to go to a nursing home. It would be impossible for us to care for her, as she needed constant care. There was no opening in Melbourne. We had to take her to Kissimmee about forty miles away. It was a new care center and a very beautiful place. When there was an opening in Melbourne we had her transferred to a Palm Bay center, much closer to home. We visited her often and would take her for rides and to McDonalds for a hamburger. She gradually grew weaker and on Sunday afternoon, March 21, 1993 she died peacefully at the age of 92; Cina, Dorothy, Jane, and myself, were with her at the nursing home.

Chapter 28

Mama Ku Ku

Our first Christmas in the bakery we met Julia Lake Kellersberger or better known as "Mama Ku Ku" which means "hello mama" in Swahele. Mama Ku Ku was a master at using adjectives and when she ran out of adjectives in the dictionary she would make up some of her own. She had a bubbling spirit and touched the lives of everyone she met. She was like a breath of fresh air; she was the wife of the famous Dr. Kellersberger who was a missionary doctor in the Belgian Congo, known today as "The Republic of Congo."

A few days before Christmas, Mama Ku Ku came in the bakery and wanted me to bake her a birthday cake for Jesus. She wanted it for a children's party. The bakeshop in downtown Melbourne was filled with late shoppers with tired faces that didn't reflect any joy of the season. Like a breath of fresh air Mama Ku Ku entered the bakery and with a loud voice said, "Merry Christmas to everyone!" The girl at the counter said, "Please take a number." "Oh, I have a number," Mama Ku Ku said cheerfully. "I am a very important VIP." Tired faces turned to smiles. "My Father," she continued, "owns many acres of land and I am the daughter of the Most High King. I want to order a birthday cake for a baby born two thousand years ago." A little girl in the store said, "I know you! You spoke in our school. You are Mama Ku Ku." Horrified the mother said, "Susan, don't call the nice lady cuckoo." Mama Ku Ku smile and explained why the children called her "Mama Ku Ku." The cake had to be special, a three tier fruitcake. She was so happy with the cake and we became the best of friends.

After her husband died, she lived alone in a cottage between the Indian River and the Atlantic Ocean. Her front door faced the river and from the back door you could see the ocean. One summer while she was traveling in the north she wanted us to stay in her home. We jumped at the chance. It was a most delightful summer, especially for David and Jonathan, as they loved the ocean for surfing.

Mrs. Kellersberger was really a very remarkable woman. She could tell missionary stories by the hour. Her favorite story was about a missionary who had a wooden leg; one who had a glass eye, and one who had false teeth. The missionary with the wooden leg was spared because the cannibals thought his leg was too tough to eat. The natives had the habit of stealing; the missionary with the glass eye solved the problem by placing his "all seeing eye" on the table in his home. The missionary with the false teeth astonished the natives by taking out his teeth and challenged them to do the same. Mrs. Kellersberger would say the three things necessary to become a successful missionary were to have a wooden leg, a glass eye, and false teeth!

"Gee Whiz!" She said with a twinkle in her eye. "It takes a lot of "G's" to be a missionary. You have to have GRACE, GRIT, GLADNESS, GOODNESS AND GUMPTION."

Chapter 29

A Movie Star

There was another remarkable woman we knew through the bakery. Her name was Jacquelyn Logan. We had invited her to our home on several occasions. She was active in the John Birch Society and sponsored many radio programs on political issues of the day. The rumor was that she was once a movie star. We never knew for sure because she never talked about it. One time she invited Cina and I to her beautiful house on the beach. We got up enough courage and asked her if she ever was in the movies. She didn't say anything but brought out a large box of photographs of herself and all the movies she was in. The movies included such stars as Clark Gable, Greta Garbo, Jackie Coohgan, and many others. Gloria Swanson was a close friend. She played the part of Mary Magdalene in Cecil de

Mille's silent version of "King of Kings." She said she never wanted to be in the movies, her desire was to be a newspaper reporter.

She needed work so she got a job in a chorus line and landed in the movies. When she lived in Hollywood she had a pet leopard, but was forced to give it up; there was quite a story about it in the newspapers. When she lived in Melbourne she had a Great Dane and I mean a great big one. He traveled everywhere she went and took up the whole back seat of her car.

Chapter 30

Teeth

When I was discharged from the Army my teeth were supposed to be in good shape, but they didn't stay that way for long. I soon had them all out. This happened when I was still with the post office. One day while eating dinner a piece of onion got caught in my throat. I ran to the bathroom and in my hurry I flushed the toilet just as the piece of onion came up, but so did my brand new teeth. They went down the drain before I knew what happened. At first I thought I just lost the lower plate, reaching for my uppers I discovered they were gone too. My dentist said he would check the city sewer department. "It happens all the time with people that drink too much." He said he could identify them, but as it turned out, out of

100 pairs of false teeth mine were no where to be found. I had the pleasure of paying double for my false teeth.

One other time while I was snorkeling in the Bahamas, struggling for air, both of my plates fell out, 20 feet down. The water was crystal clear and I could see them on the bottom. Selene, my granddaughter made one giant dive and retrieved them for me. I haven't been snorkeling since. There was one time when I was playing cards with Timmy, my grandson, I laughed so hard my upper plate went sailing across the room. Enough about teeth!

Chapter 31

What is next?

In my lifetime I can remember the first of many things. The first touring model T-Ford that my father bought was when we lived in Milaca. My dad traded a team of mules for the car. One Sunday afternoon we went to visit some neighbors and on returning the Ford wouldn't start. Finally my father went home and got a team of horses to pull the flivver home! (A model T was called a flivver)

The first electric lights were an improvement over gas and kerosene lamps. Oh yes, the party telephone! Our number was two longs rings and two short ones.

I made radio crystal sets but finally we got an Atwater Kent radio. Mert and Marge was my Mother's favorite program. My favorite program was Dr. Francis Ritter, a blind organist over KSTP St. Paul, Minnesota.

Before I was married I never heard of electric typewriters, VCR's and guys wearing earrings. Fast food was what people ate during Lent. "Chip" was a piece of wood and hardware is where you bought nails. No such word as software. Grass was something we grew in our front yard and pot was what we baked beans in. I never heard of CD's, microwaves, electric blankets or air-conditioning. I was married first and then lived together. A man walking on the moon? Impossible! F. D. R. was the first presidential election I listened to on the radio.

I remember when we would make our own ice cream from fresh fallen snow by adding sugar and vanilla; when the Sears catalog was used for toilet paper in the out house; when we made our own valentines; when milk was delivered to the front door; when the roads would be nice and muddy after a rain; when paved roads were unheard of (some had gravel); and when the mailman delivered mail twice a day.

In 1952 Cina and I bought our first TV set. We were the last on our block to buy one. I think the reason we did was to keep the kids home. They loved the "I Love Lucy" show with Lucille Ball. Now we have our first computer; I wonder what is going to be the next first. I can't imagine! Maybe it will be our first great grandchild!

Chapter 32

Dogs

My story is now going to the dogs.

While living in Milaca we had a mutt of a dog and my brother Bob and I decided it would never amount to anything. When a friend heard we wanted to give him away, he offered to take him. How lucky could we be; evidently he didn't know much about dogs.

About two months later when I was in town I decided to see my friend who took that "good for nothing" mutt off our hands. What I saw amazed me beyond words. Here was our "good for nothing" mutt doing all kinds of tricks. He was clean and well groomed, looking like a circus dog. This friend of mine saw something in this dog that I didn't see. It taught me a real lesson. Too many times I don't see the possibilities. It reminds me of a scripture verse in the Bible that says man looks at the outward appearance but God looks at the heart.

In Minneapolis I had a dog when I was in grade school. I was very much attached to him and taught him many tricks. One night during a thunderstorm he became frightened and ran away. I never saw the dog again. It about broke my heart and I decided I would never become attached to a dog again.

After my father died, my mother obtained a German police dog when she lived in north Minneapolis. She was alone a lot and appreciated the company.

I had a little Fox Terrier for company when I lived in the Ozark Mountains for a summer.

No more dogs for me until after I was married. Just before moving to Florida, a friend gave us "Annie Pie," a pure bred Boxer. In no time she became a member of the family. We had Annie Pie for many years. She died of heartworms, a disease caused by a mosquito.

When we moved to our home on Michigan Street in West Melbourne, I decided we needed a watchdog and I bought a 6-month-old German shepherd. We name her "Annie." I had fun training her. After reading all the books I could find on the subject I started her training. She learned fast, especially to "heal." Annie was a real watch- dog and fearless except for trains. Every time a train went by she would run. I took her everyday by the tracks when the trains went by. I had a time to hold her at first but each time a train went by she would be less fearful. Finally without a leash she would sit by the fast moving trains and would not move until I gave the command. The first time she had pups she got tangled up with a black Labrador by accident. The second time with a German shepherd she gave birth to 11 wonderful pups. Cina and Becky Cecchini, Cina's niece would feed them with a milk bottle and bathe them in the pond to keep the fleas off. We sold them for $50 each, except for one, which we kept and named him Rico. Our neighbor had 10 prize chickens that had just started to lay eggs; they were the neighbor's pride and joy. Annie, on one of her excursions, decided the chickens made too much noise and without being invited she broke into the hen house and killed them all. She didn't eat them, just silenced them. Our insurance covered the damage, but I was told to get rid of the dog because my insurance would not cover a second such incident. I found a man that used Annie for a night watch dog at his place of business.

Rico was a wonderful dog, very big, but not vicious like his mother. At that time Jane, my daughter, lived just across Interstate Hi-way 95 from our house. Jonathan at times would cut across the Interstate to go to Jane's instead of going around by the road. One time Rico followed Jon without him knowing it. On the way back, Rico ran ahead and while crossing the highway was hit by a truck. He died instantly. Jonathan was very fond of the dog and he had difficulty telling me what had happened. Every bone in his body was broken. It was at night and in the light of the full moon, we buried Rico under a pine tree.

Our next dog was Reca, a female Dalmatian that Jonathan got for us. She was incorrigible. No fence would hold her no matter now high. She would either climb over it or dig under it. Reca died very mysteriously and we never did discover the cause.

Our last dog was cute little "Sam," a poodle that Jane gave us. Sam was a real house pet, but Cina became allergic to dogs and we had to give Sam away. No more dogs. I still would like to have one. Maybe some day…

Chapter 33

A Trip To Italy

Cina had a deep desire to return to her native land, where she was born and grew up as a teenager. Plans were made in 1974 to fulfill that longing and to make that dream come true. Since Dorothy and Jane were already married and David was in college, we took Jonathan with us—he was going on 15. David was in his senior year at the University of Florida and he took his last semester as an extension course in Florence, Italy. We planned to be there the same time he was.

From Miami we flew to Luxembourg and by train to Zurich, Bern and on to La Chaux- de- Fonds, Switzerland to see Pina, a close friend of Cina's. Cina knew Pina at the church in Florence. Pina later married and settled in La Chaux-de-Ponds where her husband was a Waldensian

Pastor. From Switzerland we took a rapido train through the Italian Alps at sunset. The mountains were ablaze and gleaning in the colorful sunlight. It was my first view of the majestic Alps. Our first stop was in Florence and Livio; Cina's half brother met us at the station. He was a perfect image of her father. Cina was shocked to see the resemblance. After 30 years of absence there was much to catch up. We stayed with Cina's cousin, Ellina. Mario, another half-brother, and his wife also lived in Florence. They had a daughter, Betti. Betti and her husband, Paulo ran a beauty salon and they had two children, Catherina (8) and Leonardo (10).

Train service in Italy is fantastic, always on time. You could tell what city you were in by looking at the timetable. From Florence we went to Messina, and ferried across the Straights of Messina and then a train to Palermo, Sicily to see Pastor Vinay and his wife Fernanda. After 30 years many of the buildings and bridges were still in ruin.

On the way back we explored Naples and I was determined to go to Alife, a little town near Naples to see Sisto and his family, a family I had met when I was there during the war.

We took a train to Alife and everything was O. K. until the ticket agent wanted more money. We had a Eurail Pass and were told it was good all over Italy. The ticket agent demanded more money and we refused to pay anymore. By the time they decided to put us off the train we were in Alife, where we intended to go.

We looked around at the buildings and they were covered with hammer and sickle, a sign of the communist party. Very threatening! That was enough for Jonathan. He lost interest in going into town. I was determined to find Sisto's family. Jonathan refused to go further so Cina returned to Naples with Jonathan and then back to Florence. I stayed.

Walking down that street was very foreboding. The people didn't seem very friendly. I didn't recognize any of the buildings. As I walked further, I suddenly began to recognize the street and it was the street that Sisto lived on. I inquired for Angelo Zeppetelli, Sisto's father. Finally I found someone who knew where they lived. It was just a short way down the street.

I went to the door and knocked. I thought Mrs. Zeppetelli would faint. She recognized me instantly and smothered me with hugs and kisses. To tell the truth, I didn't recognize her. Before she was frail as a beanstalk, real skinny and very sad. Now she was a "Mama Mia" with a good-sized bosom and a very jolly laugh. She cooked me the most fabulous meal, steak and fried potatoes. We didn't have to say much, she didn't understand English and my Italian was rather bumpy. It didn't matter. We were happy to be together under better circumstances. She showed me the gas stove. Before they had a charcoal burner. She was happy to announce she had a refrigerator, running water and an indoor toilet.

You could see her pride when she said it was Sisto that made it possible to have all of these things. The reason we couldn't find Sisto's telephone number was because he was working with the police and had an unlisted number. Sisto lived in Milan. Sisto's father was in Milan seeing a doctor, as he was in poor health.

It was time to catch the train back to Naples. Going back I had the same trouble about paying. I played dumb and I didn't understand why it was necessary to pay more. I showed him my Eurail Pass.

Later I found out my pass was not good on that train. It was privately owned by the Socialist Party and had no connection with the main railroad.

I was happy to be back in Naples and was on a train to Florence. The conductor asked where I was going. I said to Florence and expected to be there by 10:p.m. He informed me that this was a slow train to Florence and wouldn't arrive until the next morning. What I needed was a "rapido" train to Florence. Needless to say I was off in a hurry and found the right train.

We visited all the places Cina had lived and where she went to school. From Civitavecchia by boat we went to Cagliari, Sardinia where Cina lived for many years. Cina's good friend Lina, lived in Cagliari. When back in Florence, we made a trip to Venezia (Venice) and on to Undine and Bolzano.

I wanted to see Sisto and we took off for Milano. It was a great experience meeting Sisto after 30 years. It was the first time Cina had met him; she adopted him as a brother. Sisto couldn't do enough for us, he showered us with presents. He gave me an Italian leather billfold and a wristwatch. To Cina he gave perfume and scented soaps. His wife worked for a perfume company out of Paris. Sisto had a married daughter, a teenage son and a 10-year-old boy and one grandson. His 5-year-old grandson expected to see an American soldier with uniform and all of the decorations. Instead all he saw was an old man with gray hair. He was disappointed. We all had a good laugh. Sisto tried to explain to him that I was no longer in the Army and it was many years ago when he was 14 years old, when he knew me.

I was surprised that Sisto remembered a song I had taught him many years ago. In broken English he sang, "I am so happy and here's the reason why, Jesus took my burden all away.Once my heart was heavy with the load of sin, Jesus took the burden and gave me peace within. Now I am happy as the days go by, Jesus took my sin all away…"I had to help him in some places as he sang in broken English, but he was proud to show me he remembered it. I also saw his father; he was doctoring with a specialist. We spent a couple days with Sisto and then we were on our way.

Finally we started our long journey home. When our airplane stopped in Shannon, Ireland to refuel, we caught a glimpse of the landscape. It was the greenest green I have ever seen. No wonder the Irish wear green. Arriving late at night flying over Miami we saw streets of lights, a breath taking sight. I went to rent a car but discovered my driver's license had expired. I thought I had until October 19th, my birthday, but it had expired. October 1st. Cina's driver's license had also expired. Her birthday was October 17th.

We stayed over night in a motel and called Jane. The next day Jane and Karl drove to Miami to pick us up. This was the end of a great trip.

Chapter 34

45th Wedding Anniversary 1990

Our Kids thought they should give us a vacation while we were still mobile, just in case we wouldn't be around for our 50th Anniversary. We received a letter from them saying they had planned a vacation for us:

CONGRATULATIONS!
You have been named "COUPLE OF THE YEAR" by your family.
This certificate entitles you to 3 days/ 2nights in the BIG APPLE, plus round trip air fare and tickets to an opera of your choice. (This certificate also includes 3 days of Nona-Sitting) Have fun! You deserve it!
Love, THE FAMILY July 22, 1990

New York here we come! We were on our way; flying through the clouds, it was another honeymoon. Our kids thought of everything, even reserved a room for us at the Hilton.

Tobie Cecchini, Andrea's son, our nephew, was the only person we knew in Manhattan. We called Tobie to let him know we had arrived. People—people— everywhere, when Tobie showed up it was a relief to see a familiar face. He took us to his favorite place, a Chinese restaurant in China Town. After devouring a delicious meal, we had to hurry to the Lincoln Center for our first opera. Tobie hailed a taxicab for us and thanking Tobie for the meal, we took off. We told the driver we didn't want to be late for the opera. "Don't worry," he said, "I'll get you there on time." And he did. He knew all the short cuts. Cina was thrilled to see the Lincoln Center where all of the Grand Operas are held; a dream fulfilled. We planned on hearing Pavarotti but at the last moment there was a substitute—what a disappointment. We did hear Thomas Hampson (In Don Giovanni) Cina's favorite baritone. Grand opera is part of Italian culture.

After the opera we walked to our motel about 10 blocks. We had been told to be sure and take a taxi. We felt safe even though it was midnight. The streets were crowded with people just as it is at mid-noon. We saw Les Miserables, our first Broadway show. We had box seats next to the stage. It was entertaining to see how the stage changed from scene to scene.

We took advantage of every moment, Ellis Island, the statue of Liberty and all of the great little restaurants in Manhattan, and we rode in the super elevators at the Trade Center, visited the Empire State Building. We certainly were mobile. We strolled through Central Park and the sidewalks of New York. I broke my glasses, but fortunately I had an extra pair. One place we wanted to visit, The Grand Central Station in down town Manhattan where I met Cina 45 years ago when she came to this country. At that time the station seemed huge, now it seemed so small. It brought back many sentimental and happy moments.

Yes, we had a great time—-Thanks to the family that made it possible.

Chapter 35

80th Surprise Party 1991

Dorothy and Jane had sent letters to every one we knew from Courtland Kansas, Cambridge and Madison, Wisconsin and all of our friends in Florida, asking them to send me a birthday greeting and inviting them to the surprise party. We were flooded with birthday cards. One day our mailbox was over flowing. Dorothy had a gang at her house. I thought it was a baby shower and even signed the guest list. It was a total surprise to me. The cake had 80 brightly lit candles! We sang songs from the 30's, like "You are my Sunshine," "Let me call you Sweetheart," "Red Sails in the Sunset," and "Among my Souvenirs."

"These are the real best years!" so they say…

Chapter 36

Puerto Rico—-1992

The Teen Alternative was Pastor Tim Heath's dream of sending teenagers to a foreign missionary field as Teen Missionaries during summer vacation. In 1992 Pastor Tim's dream was to send 10 teenagers to Camp Caribbean in Juana Diez Puerto Rico where Grace Missions has a camp. Cina and I volunteered to go as cooks. Kit Edwards and Bruce Menconi were the leaders and 10 teenagers from different Grace Churches made up the entourage. Each one had to raise their support. Our church put on a yard sale to help raise money for the project. Cina and I put on a skit to advertise the yard sale. We did this one Sunday morning before church. It was a Gracie Allen and George Burns episode.

Ernie:	Did you know that next Saturday May 13th the Grace Bible Church is having a garage sale?

Ernie: Did you know that next Saturday May 13th the Grace Bible Church is having a garage sale?

Cina: Are you selling the yard?

Ernie: No, Gracie, we are not selling the yard. You see the church doesn't have a garage, so we don't call it a garage sale, we call it a yard sale.

Cina: You mean you sold the garage?

Ernie: No, Gracie, we didn't sell the garage. I will try to explain it to you and make it real simple. It is like this. The people donate things to the church and we sell them. For instance, Eldora is donating a riding lawn mover. It is in very good shape and if we sell it just for $200 it would be a steal.

Cina: Who's stealing?

Ernie: Nobody is stealing anything. It is just an expression. It's a bargain or a good deal or it is a good buy!

Cina: Good Bye! Who's leaving?

Ernie: We are with the teen alternative to Puerto Rico to help the missionaries. The money we make will be used for the trip.

Cina: I know. Money comes and money goes!

Ernie: In this case it is for a good cause. Now Gracie I want you to remember three things. Next Saturday At 8:00 o'clock is the men's fellowship breakfast and after that the yard sale. The young people are also having a car wash.

Cina: Yes, cleanliness is next to Godliness!

Ernie: First is the breakfast and then the yard sale and the car wash, and Gracie if you have anything you want to donate to the yard sale—you know, something nice, like an antique, something very old.

Cina: Holds up a (FOR SALE) sign in front of Ernie.

Ernie: OK Gracie, you can't sell me! I want you to remember three things for next Saturday. Remind me about the breakfast and the yard sale and especially the car wash.

Cina: OK George!

From Miami we flew to San Juan and then took a bus to the camp at Juana Diez. It wasn't all work. We visited the rain forest in San Juan and explored many caves. The caves had this sign—-

- FROM the cave you will only take pictures
- IN the cave you will only leave your footprints
- IN the cave you will only kill time.

We got the message.

We attended The Grace Church in Ponce where Trixie Hammond was the missionary. I made a lot of home made bread by hand…and the kids devoured it! The sand on the beach was black as coal. We had to take a sample home with us. We were in Puerto Rico from June 22 to July 30, 1992.

Nineteen hundred ninety two was crammed with many festive activities for Cina and me. In June and July it was the Puerto Rico experience at Camp Caribbean in Juanna Diez. Before going to Puerto Rice we had decided to sell our home in West Melbourne and to build a smaller house in Palm Bay. We found the perfect lot on Candlestick Avenue and Holiday Builders assured us it would be finished in three months. We moved in a few days before Thanksgiving Day. November 1992.

Then came the Caribbean Cruise. Shawn, our granddaughter, who worked on the Royal Caribbean Cruise Line, surprised us with a cruise during the holiday season, between Christmas and New Year. Christmas Day we spent in the middle of the Caribbean. It seemed strange not to be home for Christmas. A friend, Trixie Hammond, a missionary in Ponce, went with us. Like delinquent children on a floating hotel we had the time of our lives. We feasted day and night and explored every island where the ship stopped. After the cruise, we went to Ponce and stayed with Trixie to bring in the New Year, Spanish style. The young people went house-to-house singing carols and eating special holiday goodies with a Puerto Rican flavor.

MONARCH OF THE SEAS

DECEMBER 1996

Our grandchildren 1996
(Back row) Shawn, Chanda, David, Shannon, Tim, Desiree, Selene
(Front row) Brooke, Amy, Joshua, Jordy, and Breanna

Chapter 37

Weddings and More Weddings

Shannon was the first of the grand children to be married. On July 10,1993 Shannon Olsen became Mrs. Phillip Hayes. They were married and now live in Melbourne.

Melbourne High School and Eau Gallie High School came together. Shannon went to Mel High and Phil went to Eau Gallie High, a rival high school, and they met through a mutual friend. It was love at first sight! However there was a drawback. Phil's dad lived in Sacramento, California and after graduating from high school, Phil headed for the west coast to attend the University of California at Davies. The separation was too much for Shannon—after graduating from High School, and a year of college, she flew to Sacramento, rented an apartment and worked as a nanny until Phil graduated. After graduating from Davis, with flying colors, a great job opened for Phil in Florida with Sun Bank in Titusville, Florida and then with Huntington National Bank in Melbourne.

Who knows when they will need a "nursery".

August 7,1993——Selene Meier became Mrs. Roger Boutin

Selene and Roger graduated from the same college, Florida State, so there was no rivalry. I remember Selene saying Roger was the only decent fellow she had met –and evidently Roger saw something worthwhile in Selene and before we knew it wedding bells were ringing. It was one of those divine appointments.

Selene and Shannon are cousins and they grew up together, they have much in common; the same age and were married in the same year. Now the question is who will be a mother first!

They were married August 7, 1993 and are now living in Tampa. Roger has a business position and Selene is a nurse practitioner.

November 16, 1996—Cherrie Reyes became Mrs. Timothy Olsen. The couple was married at Grace Bible Church in Palm Bay by Timothy's cousin, Rick Englert officiating. It was a beautiful ceremony and the reception was held out doors at Jane Meier's home at 2701 Michigan Street, West Melbourne. Incidentally that was our home at one time. Unfortunately the relationship didn't last.

September 27, 1997—Lisa Odom became Mrs. David Meier.

It was a case of school rivalry. David graduated from Florida State and Lisa was a strong Florida Gator. David's good judgment finally won out; he chose Lisa from a long list of admirers. It was love forever!

David and Lisa's wedding was a day to remember. In the morning Cina and I went to Julia Irvins' wedding at Orchid Island. Julia was a close friend to the family and a schoolmate of Shawn Olsen, my granddaughter. After a long reception we hurried home, rested a little and then off to David's wedding in Melbourne. After a beautiful ceremony, we heard the famous words, "Meet Mr. and Mrs. David Meier." At the reception David's fraternity friends put on quite a show— a demonstration of energy. Everyone was dancing included Cina and me; couples were illuminated according to years of marriage, starting with Silver Anniversary— many couples sat down—40 years many more couples sat down. Golden Anniversary, 50 years, Cina and I were the only couple left dancing. We received a roaring ovation!

It was a beautiful wedding and after the reception at the Hilton, the couple enjoyed a Caribbean cruise.

August 5, 2000 Chanda Hedges became Mrs. William Griese.

Merle, David Hedges' wife made a gorgeous three tiered wedding cake for Chanda, but made a fatal mistake of making the icing with butter, which can prove to be disastrous, especially in August. The warm humid air softened the butter and the top two layers started to slide and fell to the floor. The cake was decorated with silk and real flowers and also roses made from icing. Fortunately the bottom layer stayed intact and Merle with her artistic touch made it look as though nothing happened. The cake was delicious and most people didn't know the difference. I know I didn't until Merle told me what happened. The bottom tier was a large three-layer cake and everybody in the reception had a piece. It was just one of those little things that happens at weddings. Jonathan and Shannon sang a wedding song and Jonathan and Roberto Alonso rendered a stirring Spanish song. After the ceremony we heard the famous words, "You may now kiss the Bride. I introduce to you Mr. and Mrs. William Griese!!" Chanda was a beautiful bride, charming and dainty!

Dorothy and Shawn took over the decorations at the Captain's House in Palm Bay and managed the food with the help of the rest of the family. I made homemade bread for the gang.

Chapter 38

A Surprise 50th Wedding Anniversary – 1945-1995

"Cina, what ever happened to some of these pictures that are missing?" I asked. "I have no idea," she replied. It was a puzzle that was bothersome for sometime; disturbing to have so many sentimental photos just vanish, a mystery not solved for a whole year. For a year our family planned a surprise party for our 50th wedding anniversary. Very cleverly they had taken pictures from our photo album to piece together our life for the past 50 years. David, our son, had the pictures put on slides and using the overhead projector, he narrated the whole story.

The celebration took place at the Port Malabar Country Club. We were told it was a birthday party for Barry. Dorothy and Paul took Cina and me to the country club and as we opened the door we were showered with greetings.

HAPPY ANNVERSARY GRANDPA AND NONNA!

My sisters, Hazel and Eunice and my niece, Milly Beggs were here without our knowledge. What a wonderful added surprise!

We had no wedding cake at our wedding, as it was wartime, so the Pastor made apple doughnuts. 50 years later—there it was, a three tiered wedding cake, beautifully decorated; also the apple doughnuts. My first question was, "Where are the apple doughnuts?" And there they were!

It was Hazel's 89th birthday and we sang "Happy Birthday." The five youngest grandchildren; Chanda, Joshua, Jordy, Amy and Brooke recited a poem. *"We love you not only for what you* are, *but what I am when I am with you."* After reciting the poem, they showered Cina and me with roses. Then all our children and grandchildren sang, "Life is an Ocean—the whole crew is here."

Jonathan was scheduled to sing, but because he had a black eye, he asked a friend to sing; he sang "The Old Rugged Cross" and "In The Garden."

Then came the slide pictures of our 50 years of life together narrated by David. A delicious meal was served, but I must confess I was too excited to eat. After 50 years we finally got to cut our wedding cake. Phil interviewed all of the guests. Many friends from the church were there. It was a time of fellowship and rejoicing and all had a good time.

The next day Cina, Milly, and I drove to Milaca, Minnesota to celebrate my oldest sister, Pearl's 100th birthday.

Paul, Ernie, Dorothy, and Cina 50th wedding anniversary surprise

Eunice and Hazel   Ernie and Milly

Our 50th Wedding
Anniversary
1995

Chapter 39

The year 1998

Cina and I went to visit our good friends, Craig and Kathleen Burleson who lived in Virginia near Winchester. We left the Melbourne airport at 7 AM Thursday morning, May 21,1998, transferred in Atlanta to Washington D. C. We stayed with the Burleson's until Saturday morning and then we went to our time-share in Basye, Virginia. Cina wasn't able to walk much and her cough was getting worse. Friday afternoon we went back to the Burleson's. Sunday we went to the church where Craig was the pastor and we enjoyed meeting the people. Cina's health did not improve. Monday we returned to Melbourne and when transferring in Atlanta we had to go to the far end of the terminal. Cina couldn't walk that far and we were running out of time. I helped Cina to a bench—I had to get a wheelchair—fast! I turned around and there was a wheelchair! I marveled about that many times, just when we needed one, it was a miracle! The Lord provides. We arrived in Melbourne at 7 PM and Jane and Dorothy were there to meet us.

The next morning I took Cina to see Doctor Todd and he sent her to the Palm Bay Hospital for lung ex-rays. At first the doctor thought Cina might have tuberculosis and he had us wearing masks because tuberculosis is very contagious. After more test and x-rays, it was determined it was not tuberculosis but a fast growing cancer. Many of the family members were in the hospital and Dr. Todd requested we meet in the waiting room. The doctor's face showed that he was very concerned and I could tell he had bad news to tells us. The doctor started by saying, "This is the hardest thing I have ever had to do." He took a deep breath and continued, "Your wife has a rapid growing lung cancer and is too far along for treatment." The family was in shock. We had no idea it was that serious. I asked the doctor, "How long does she have?" The doctor responded without hesitation, "I would say she has about a month to live." I was overwhelmed with shock and grief and hid my face in my hands.

"The cancer is so far advanced I do not recommend treatment," the doctor was saying, "because it would only add to her discomfort. The best we can do is to make her as comfortable as possible. You can take her home and I will arrange for Hospice of Health First to take over.

Lung cancer, how could it be? She never smoked in her life; even the doctor had no clue. Surely the doctor must be mistaken. She was always in good health, very careful about her diet and read every label. Cancer was the last thing we thought possible. A couple of months before Cina had a complete physical examination and the report were satisfactory. I could not accept it, but I had to face reality. The doctor had reported his diagnosis. Should we tell Cina? We decided not to at this time.

After I gained my composure, I went to Cina and said, "I have some good news, the doctor said we could take you home." Cina very gracefully responded and was happy to leave the hospital. I knew she knew what was going on but she showed no sign of stress or despair.

It was a pleasure to wait on Cina. I always loved Cina but now I really realized how much I loved her. I cooked her favorite foods and I prepared plenty of vegetables and fruit. We had just replaced the carpet with tile that made it easier to get around on a chair with rollers. Cina rested quite comfortably for several days but each day her coughing increased. When I called the nurse, she would come, whenever I needed her, no matter what time it happened to be. For the next 15 days Jane and Dorothy stayed day and night. The rest of the family was close by and Guido and Andrea, Cina's brothers were here from Eau Claire, Wisconsin.

Shannon and Selene, our granddaughters were pregnant at the time and Cina was excited to become a great grandmother. She wanted to knit some booties for the babies—she was never able to make them. Each day she grew weaker and was unable to swallow and eventually could not talk. Hospice provided a hospital bed and I put it next to my bed. Jane and I took turns watching her. One time I dozed off and all of a sudden I felt someone tugging on my pajamas. At first I thought it was Jane but it was Cina trying to get my attention. I could tell she wanted to talk, but no sound came. I talked to her. I told her how much I loved her and the family was here. I read to her the first three chapters of Ephesians that she loved so much. "He made us accepted in the Beloved. In Him we have redemption through His blood, the forgiveness of sins, according to the riches of His Grace." She was at rest and went back to sleep. The following day at 4 PM Cina opened her eyes and she became very alert. The family gathered around her bed. I mentioned everybody's name and Jonathan played the guitar and we sang several hymns. Cina communicated to us through her eyes. Finally I said, "Cina we love you and it is all right to let go." She closed her eyes and took one final breath. "Precious in the sight of God is the death of His Saints."

The children and grandchildren took charge of the memorial service, July 8,1998 at Grace Bible Church in Palm Bay, Florida. They sang many of Cina's favorite hymns. Jonathan played his guitar and sang "The Old Rugged Cross' and "In The Garden." They closed with everyone singing, "When we all get to Heaven, what a day of rejoicing it will be." Chanda played, "Joyful, Joyful, We Adore Thee," on her violin. Brooke accompanied her cousin on the piano and Breanna recited a verse. Our son David gave the eulogy. Phillip wrote a poem about Nonna:

Il Fiore Nonna
Feel the gentle breeze
Our Hearts call for her tonight
The flower, her grace she lifted us
The beauty, her life she gifted us

Hear the rain patter the sea tonight
Lost in thoughts are we tonight
The flower, her love it meant to us
The color, her spirit, her words to us
Touch the flower with me tonight
Smile and laugh, she's free tonight
The flower, her caress it goes over us
Then dream, her memory it lives in us.

Sharon Irvin, Karl Meier, and Shannon gave some words of appreciation. Pastor Doug Hadley read the scriptures. Refreshments were served and we met our many friends.

Chapter 40

Great-Grandchildren

Breanna is the daughter of Cherrie Reyes from a previous marriage, but we consider her as one of the flock. Timothy cares for her as one of his own. She is a beautiful ten-year-old girl and we all love her.

Desiree Nicole Olsen, the first of the great-grandchildren was born July 12, 1996 in Melbourne, Florida. It not only made Cina and I great-grandparents but now Dorothy was a grandma and Paul a grandpa. That was hard to believe! Our first baby a grandmother! It made us all happy to have a baby in the family again—Brooke Hedges was the last baby and that was 10 years ago.

Eleanore Rue Hayes, the second of our great-grandchildren, was born November 21, 1998 in Melbourne, Florida. Cina was happy to know she would be a great-grandmother again. She always knitted booties for all of the babies and had me purchase yarn for the booties, however she never was able to make them because of her health. Cina went to be with the Lord, 4 months before Elli was born. Elli was named after her great grandmother, Eleanore Olsen, Paul's mother.

Cina Madelyn Boutin, the third of our great-grandchildren. She was born January 16, 1999 in Tampa, Florida. Cina was ecstatic to know another great-grandchild was on the way. Since she wasn't able to make the booties, a woman from the church, Mrs. Powell, made them after Elli and Cina were born. Roger and Selene asked me if I would mind if they called their baby, "Cina." I was more than happy; I call her "Cina mia and Cina Bella." Roger's mother's name was Madelyn. Baby Cina was named after her grandmother and great grandmother.

Another Great Grandchild

April Marie Griese was born October 5, 2001. She weighed four pounds, 14 ounces. After a week in the hospital, she was able to go home. Chanda and Billy became professional parents over night. Jonathan was strictly in shock that his granddaughter could be so small and that he was a grandpa! April Marie is very tiny, beautiful, adorable, and became the center of attention at my 90th birthday party. She was only a month old. I had to take a back seat—she was the celebrity for the evening! April Marie is my fourth great grandchild.

I planned on having my book published and completed by now. But, as things sometimes have a way of being 'put on hold', I now have another great grandchild.

Chloe Tais Boutin was born March 18, 2002. She weighed 7 pound 6 ounces. Proud daddy Roger, happy Nonna Jane, and jubilant cousin Shawn were on hand to experience the birth. Shawn was a little disappointed there was "no dramatic" action. She heard stories of giving birth but everything went so fast and so smooth. I continue to have another Tais in my life.

No picture yet, but Phillip and Shannon Hayes just found out they are having a baby boy expecting to be born in August 2002. How will he adapt to his sister Elli and all his female cousins?

David and Lisa Meier are expecting their first child September 2002. Lisa is doing fine and we all are waiting for this blessed event.

Paul, Dorothy, Tim, Shawn and Shannon Olsen
1980

Paul and Dorothy Olsen
2001

Desiree, Tim Olsen and Breanna

Shawn and Joe Fijol

Shannon, Eleanore and Phillip Hayes

Karl, Jane, David and Selene Meier
1976

Officer Jane Meier

Karl Meier, Lisa and David Meier, Jane Meier, Selene and Roger Boutin
2001

Roger, Cina and Selene Boutin

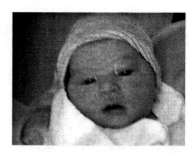

Chloe Tais Boutin
(2-18-2002)

Lisa and David Meier

David, Merle, Jordy and Brooke Hedges
1989

Brooke, Jordy, David and Merle Hedges
2002

Jonathan Hedges

Joshua Hedges

Billy, April and Chanda Griese

Amy Hedges

Guido, Teresa (Cina) and Andrea Cecchini

Our second home
Madison, Wisconsin
37 Walter St.

Chapter 41

Invasion of Italy—2001

For two years my family had been busy making plans to visit Florence, Italy, where Cina, my wife, was born and lived. They wanted to experience the life in Italy, especially the Tuscany Valley, the country of olives and grapes with its apricot colored buildings with faded green shutters, ancient tile roofs and a romantic iron balcony on the second level. Another incentive was the good Italian food. They searched on the Internet for the best deals and it paid off. After many e-mails and telephone calls, Joe, Shawn's fiancé, made many of the reservations. Joe is the only person I know that can talk on two cell phones, send an e-mail, and type, all at the same time.

Seven different families were in the entourage and each had their own agenda. Some traveled extensively in Italy and some went to England,

France, and Germany. By prearrangement, they all met in Florence at the appointed time. They visited the Waldensian church where Cina and I were married and they visited the Seminary where the 15th Evac. Hospital, my outfit, was stationed. It was very emotional for me just to hear them talk about it. It was a happy time of my life. No, I didn't go to Florence with them; it was too much traveling for me. Some day I would like to go and stay in one place and bask in memories of Florence.

The high light of the whole trip was the dinner with the 35 Italian relatives. The relatives from America consisted of the following; Paul, Dorothy, David, Merle, and their children, Jordy and Brooke, Shannon, Phil, and their daughter, Elli, (2 years old) Selene, Roger, David M., Lisa, Shawn, Joe, Guido and Linda, 17 in all. David turned a little pale when he received the tab! Some of the others came to his rescue. After two and three weeks of traveling they all returned home safely, with thousands of pictures!!

Chapter 42

Samson

Brooke Hedges, my granddaughter, decided I needed a puppy. One day Brooke and her mother came over to my house with a beautiful little sheltie, a miniature collie, but after a couple of days they decided it wasn't very healthy; they returned the puppy.

One day while riding with Brooke and her father, we saw a sign posted on a telephone pole, "Shelties for sell." They decided to check it out. I debated whether or not I really wanted a dog. Brooke seemed to think I did. We went to the address. The Lady informed us she did have one puppy left, a six weeks old sheltie for $300. The little girl of the family had already named the puppy," Samson." Samson looked very healthy with a likable sparkle in his eyes and the right color for a sheltie, tan with black and white markings. I still couldn't make up my mind. I didn't feel right about David paying that much money for a dog for me. David said he had another ad we could check out. We left the house and drove about a block away when Brooke asked me, "Grandpa, didn't you like Samson?" I had to admit I did and I thought he was very lovable. Brooke said, "I think we should vote for Samson." The vote was 2 to 1. That settled it; David turned the car around, went back to the house and paid the asking price for the dog. Now I had a dog and thanks to Brooke for helping me to make up my mind. Samson has been a blessing and a lot of company. We became the best of friends. Thanks Brooke!

Chapter 43

Candlestick Avenue
1992—2001

Candlestick Avenue, a street one block long gives off much light—because of the good neighbors. Randy Carmean, Sharon his wife and their two delightful girls, Ashley and Nicola filled an empty spot in my heart after Cina's passing. Then there was Zack, Chandra, and Jesalyn Dyess, and Dustin, Steve, and Sunny. They called me Grandpa. I had a lot of adopted grandchildren on Candlestick Avenue.

Every Tuesday Randy and I would have lunch together. Sometimes I would cook, other times Randy would treat me to Mexican or Chinese food. Thursday night was Awana night. We would pack the kids in Randy's van and take them to Grace Bible Church for fun and games, but most of all to learn Bible verses. It was a challenge but worth it. Pat and Bill, who lived across the street, kept their yard manicured, and Pat grew many flowers and colorful plants. Then there was Weda—the nurse, Dustin's mother, who kept me in check and there was never a dull moment!

Sundays I would pick up Zack, Chandra and Jesalyn for Sunday School and Church. Zack said the reason he was saved was because I kept after him to accept Christ as his Savior. My heart rejoiced! Christmas 1999 Zack gave me a plaque —"There's no place like home, except at Grandpa's"

My nine years on Candlestick was a happy time, but now it is time for me to go. I am selling my house and moving in with Jane my daughter in West Melbourne. I will miss my friends on Candlestick!

490 Candlestick Ave. Palm Bay, Florida

Chapter 44

Next To The Final Chapter

I call this next to the final chapter of my life because I am in good health at 90 and going strong. Someone else will have to write the final chapter.

My beloved wife, Cina died July 6, 1998—4pm, three months before her 75th birthday and one month before our 53rd Wedding Anniversary. When I said she died, I mean the "earthly house she lived in died; she is still alive. Absent from the body is to be present with The Lord. My authority is the Holy Scriptures. Miraculously God has preserved His Word in written form so we can read it and pass it on to the next generation. It has never been revised because it was perfect to start with. It has stood the test of time—two to six thousand years. The Bible is the most beautiful poetry ever written, true to history and science. It was not written to be a scientific textbook but it contains true science; the earth is a sphere, life comes from life and after their kind, just a few examples. It was written to show our God is a just God and is The God of all grace. Blessed is the person that has experienced the reality of God's grace.

To think that such an evil force such as Adoph Hitler and a Second World War was the way God used to bring us together, from the prairie State of Kansas to the most beautiful city of Florence Italy. When I entered the Army, I certainly had no idea that I would fall in love with an Italian girl, yes; it was love at first sight. Every young man has his own idea of his dream girl, I had mine and Cina fulfilled it to a tee.

How can I describe Cina—beauty is in the eye of the beholder and to me she was the one and only one for me! Love can over come many obstacles, and arguments; no doubt we had some, but I can't remember any of them.

Cina never wanted to wear expensive clothes, but what ever she wore looked expensive. Even in the way she rode a bicycle she had dignity and charm. She never visited a beauty salon, not necessary; she had just the natural wave in her hair. Oh yes, she used a little lipstick and her favorite perfume was "4711". She always knew what I would give her on her birthday—a large bottle of "4711". Her humor—at the cutting edge, sort of dry, but it was always there. My wife, "The All Knowing Woman."

The following is a poem we received from Mrs. E. R. Foulk, who lived in Madison, Wisconsin.

"Cina!" what a pretty name and how it fits you too:
It's easy to understand why Ernie is in love with you.
Your face lights up with laughter, your smiles as sweet as spring.
And even the birds are envious when they hear you sing.
I like to think that you are my friend, both trusted and sincere.
You bring me special happiness whenever you are near.
I know you loved Florence, Italy, in the land across the sea,
But I hope you've found happiness over here with Ernie
For you have both been blessed with God's great gift of love.
May you find your greatest joy, when you meet with Him above.

Chapter 45

The summer of 1998

The summer of 1998 was the year of the great forest fires in Florida. The smoke filled the air for days; smoldering peat fires, and no rain was in sight. We had gone several months without a drop of rain. The very hour Cina passed from this world to the next the sky opened and released much needed rain. David said that it was a sign for him that some one special had left this earth.

How do you say good-bye to some one you love? You don't. She will always be with us.

I went through many dark hours of loneliness and sleeplessness. I could not sleep—the nights were so long. We do not grieve like those who have no hope, but we do grieve their absence. Ephesians 3:16 gave me great strength, —-"according to the riches of His Glory, to be strengthened with might by His Spirit." Cina sang a song many times that became very meaningful to me.

God understands your sorrow, He sees the falling tear, and whispers
I am with you, then falter not, nor fear.
He understands your longing, your deepest grief He shares;
Then let Him bear your burden, He understands, and cares.

Cina took great pride in her grandchildren. The following poem she wrote shows her love and concern, not only for her grandchildren but for all the children she came in contact with.

"Holy Father, help me as I teach the boys and girls, that I may teach in such a way so that they may learn to love you and obey you. As I teach, may I be aware at all times that it is your Word I am teaching, that I am handling the truth. Thank you for all I have received from you through Christ, your Beloved Son and my Savior."

Your Servant Cina

Cina and I enjoyed playing games of all kinds and when we were alone it was Skip-bo, three to thirteen, rumaque, and all kinds of rummy. Cina was an expert and had the games down to a science. She usually won. When we played skip-bo with Guido and Linda it was for blood!

When Cina's Mother, Tais, died in April 14, 1993 Cina wrote this poem;
Dear Lord
You truly are the God of Hope
You are the one that can put
Muscles and flesh on the dry
Bones, you can put your Spirit in
Them and bring them to life.
Is anything too hard for you?
I know it is not, for you are the
Giver of life, out of nothing-you
Bring all things to be
Therefore I can trust you because
You are able and your actions are
Not motivated by duty but by love.
May my heart and lips praise you at
all times.
Thankfully, your redeemed one,
Cina

Cina was a student and she loved to write. Here are some more of her writings that I found in her scrapbook.

***

The 40th chapter of Isaiah

***

Today I read the 40th chapter of Isaiah, and it was
Like I read it for the first time!
Was it the first time?
It couldn't be, for I have read the Bible through
Several times, and the book of Isaiah I have also read by itself.
Yet, today it seemed, like for the first time, its beauty

And magnitude overwhelmed me.
To whom would be liken to our God?
I think of the many artists who have tried to portray
Christ, yet Christ was a man, but Christ was also
God.
There must have been something in Him that no artist
Could ever capture that "something" that pertains to God
Alone.
His power, His strength, His intelligence, His tender
Love, who can sculpture that, or paint it on canvas?
But if not with our eyes, we can experience the fruit
Of these attributes when we entrust our lives to Him,
The Eternal One.
"Those that hope in the Lord will renew their strength
they will soar on wings like eagles." vs. 31.
Overwhelmed Cina

This is a beautiful poem that Brooke Hedges wrote about her Grandmother Cina. Brooke wrote this when she was eleven years old.

Slipping Tears
By: Brooke Hedges
As a tear slipped from my eye-from my cheek
My heart sunk, became weak.
I entered a forbidden place
As another tear slipped from my face
A place of sorrow a place of woe
A place I promised I would not go.
As this gorgeous, incredible grandmother slipped through my small fingers
I realized to me she was everything…Nonna, teacher, an angel, and a singer
As I held my glum broken heart
I knew it was our time to depart
To Jesus "hello"
To her beloved Italy, "so long."
To perfect Heaven a soft whisper, "hi."
Now two tears to me "good-bye"
slipped from my solemn face
Down to my glove in threaded with lace.
I lifted my glove and gently wiped the tears from my eye,
I had entered the forbidden place.
I started to cry.
She had said please…no tears.
As I thought about this, several tears fell from my chin;
Then I started to remember when—
We were together locked in each other's arms,
This lifted my heart, now I knew there was no more mourn.
I then realized she is now in a much better place,
Now gazing with a smile
No more tears slipped from my face.
To a perfect mother, grandmother, wife, aunt, angel, and many
many more!

Cina's Prayer
Thank you Lord for your
Word.
It goes to my heart like the
Dew on the dry land,
Just like the first time I heard
Your Word—It never loses
It's wonders. This too is your
"Grace."
I thank you and I love you.
Cina

Chapter 46

September 11, 2001

"Dad," an excited phone call from Dorothy, "are you watching TV? Something is going on. A plane is being hijacked." I quickly turned on the TV just as the first plane crashed in the 110-story World Trade Center Tower in New York City. Before I could comprehend what was going on, I saw the second plane plunge into the second tower and explode, filling the sky with a huge ball of smoke. Both towers collapsed after the terrorist attack. Minutes later a third plane slammed into the Pentagon in Washington D. C. The Fox News reported Terror—U. S. cities under siege. Cal Thomas, a reporter, said "Sept. 11, 2001—another day that will live in infamy." Before the day was over we heard about the fourth plane that crashed somewhere in Pennsylvania. We are all on the front lines; a day I will long remember.

War was declared on Terror.

Chapter 47

October 19th - 90th Birthday Celebration

You can call it a celebration because that is what it was—a week of celebrating. First I was surprised at church, they sang some of my favorite hymns. Dorothy said the hymn she remembers me singing was "At the Cross, At the Cross, Where I First Saw the Light." To top it off we had a potluck dinner and a huge birthday cake.

Friday October 19th we were at Dorothy's. The food was delicious and Shannon's German chocolate birthday cake made a big hit. We played "Pit," a game we enjoyed playing when we felt like making lot of noise. After that came the trivia game where Lisa and David Meier were in charge, with questions from potluck to travel and Disney World and "Roots" in between. The game was entertaining and educational. "What sport did Phil excel in High School?" (Swimming) What year did the Hedges Bakery open in downtown Melbourne? (1964)—and many more. We were divided into two teams. My team won—950 - 345.

Saturday evening the gang went to David and Merle's for a gala formal dinner, where we all dressed up. The furniture in the living room was removed and Merle had small tables set up with flowers and a small-framed picture of me on each one. — Balloons all over the place—A chef was hired and the prime roast was out of this world. All the food was the best and there was another birthday cake, Merle's famous carrot, pump-kin, and pineapple cake with cheese icing.

The great surprise was to see Milly Beggs, my niece, and her daughter Cathy from Lake City, Florida. They had arrived unknown to me. I won-dered what surprise they would have. I can always expect one. Guido, Cina's brother, came but I knew he was coming, no surprise.

After the fabulous meal, Jonathan played his guitar and sang a number of songs. Brooke read a beautiful poem she had written just for me. Then they had a "Roast" for me. Now, do you think it was nice for my children and grandkids to roast their 90-year-old father and grandpa? They enjoyed it and so did I. The next morning we all enjoyed a brunch at the "Black Pearl" on the beach.

***

My Grandpa's 90!
By Brooke Hedges

My Grandpa's 90! Me oh my!
He doesn't look but 35
He sure has a lot stored in that ol' head

And he can still bake a great loaf of bread!
He's a hard opponent in Rumi cube and chess
I think he might just be the best!
It's a rare occasion when he's not the winner
And you can always count on him to make an excellent dinner
He can make all sorts of stuff like pasta and cake
And he can always make me smile, a hug, a joke, that's all it takes!
He's also a real sportsman, and don't be laughing
Because it's true, he went white water rafting!
He's also a biblical scholar, and has a lot of faith
And that is what sustains him and keeps in that race.
My Grandpa's great, and he does lots and lots
He even looked after me, when I had the chicken pox
Well, he's the perfect grandpa, and that will stay the same
And I will always love him, and that will never change!

Chapter 48

Hold The Press...Shawn and Joe are getting Married

Shawn became Mrs. Joseph Fijol November 3, 2001.

Shawn Teresa Olsen and Joseph Michael Fijol were married in the backyard at the home of David and Merle Hedges, 9 Cache Cay Drive, Vero Beach, Florida.

After working for seven years as a purser, an activity organizer and then as a computer instructor on the Royal Caribbean Cruise Line, Shawn was introduced to Joe by a mutual friend. It was love at first sight for Joe and he called his mother and said, "Ma, I have met a girl!" "I know, you have met a lot of girls," she chuckled. "No, you don't understand," he stammered. "She is "The Girl." Later when Joe's mother met Shawn for the first time, she agreed, "She is The Girl for you."

The romance started slowly at first but each time they dated, the fiber of their relationship grew thicker and stronger, until the wedding date was decided.

Michelle, a number 4 rated Hurricane was churning up the coast of Cuba, headed for the Florida Keys. The forecast was not favorable for an outdoor wedding.

The day before the wedding, it rained. The day after the wedding it rained. The day of the wedding it was a glorious sunny day, a cloudless sky, ideal for a garden wedding. Some said they were lucky to have a beautiful day between two stormy days, but the bride knew better. Many were praying for a nice day and their prayers were answered.

Shawn and Joe creatively planned their wedding to the smallest detail. Gooding's catering service took charge, setting up round tables and cooking the food; Wellington chicken, their famous smashed potatoes and grilled vegetables. Shrimp and snacks were plentiful and Merle Hedges, David's wife, made a fantastic wedding cake.

Rick Englert, Shawn's cousin was the officiating minister. Shannon Hayes, Shawn's sister sang "Time To Say Good-bye" in loving memory of Cina Hedges, Art and Eleanore Olsen (Shawn's grandparents), and Phillip Lynett (Joe's grandfather). Shannon also sang, "Be Thou My Vision," "I Am Nothing," "I Need You," and " Something Good." Shannon sang beautifully and was much enjoyed and appreciated. Then came the pronouncement of Husband and Wife with the stirring music of Handel's Halleluiah Chorus. It was a good start for a happy marriage.

Epilogue

Grandfather's Exhortation and Prayer For His Children and their Children's Children

Every tree has a meaning and ends up on the paper I am writing on. Each drop of rain has a purpose; to make the tree grow. Even the flowers have their place, just for a day and then they fade, and die, but the human spirit lives on. You have a meaning. Each day is a challenge. It is up to you to choose, to choose life, not defeat and death. Life is precious. Just ask the person that has been told by their doctor that they have only a month to live. This is a beautiful world also it is a junky world. There is good and there is evil. We soon find out we cannot trust in ourselves. The everlasting arms of the God who made us are there to protect us.

Divinity was channeled to mere man when Christ Jesus came to this earth. Christ's earthly life proved He could be our high priest, our advocate, and a mediator between God and man. Christ can be touched with the feelings of our infirmities. He was in all points tried as we are yet without sin. Christ's death, burial, and resurrection, are the means, through faith, of our becoming right with God. Human goodness cannot make a person right with God. The God who made the world, the Judge over all mankind, became our Savior and has power to forgive sin. This is the greatest transaction in the world. God takes our sin and gives us Christ's righteousness, our passport to heaven. All God asks of us is to trust Him and be thankful and show gratitude, and obey. The Bible, God's Word, rightly divided is my authority.

You might say you are not interested. As I said before, it is up to you to choose. You are what you believe. My prayer for you is that you will anchor your soul in the "Solid Rock," the "Word of God".

Some day when you have nothing else to do, curl up in an easy chair and read these pages and relive my life. Just think if I had never been born how different things would be. These pages would be blank. Nothing! But the Great Designer had a plan, and it included you. Be thankful. Loves rejoices in the "Truth." God loves you and so do I———-

Your Father, Grandfather, and Great Grandfather—Ernest R. Hedges 2002

An Afterword

By Dorothy (Dotti) Olsen and Jane Meier

Don't you love looking at photo albums? Pictures tell stories of special events, vacations, fun times, sad times; people we know and love. But have you ever gotten into the attic, or found boxes stored away with old photo albums of family and just wish the pages could introduce you to your aunt or uncle, a grandmother or grandfather? Have you wondered what they were like? What they did? What their thoughts were? How life was during that period of history? We are so fortunate to have a father who took the time to journal his life experiences so that some day when future generations pick-up that old photo album, they will be able to relive those pictures in their grandfather's own words.

One day, our brother David approached dad and said Dad, I do not know anything about your family history, fill me in. That was 10 years ago! And so Dad, at the age of 80, began his journey back in time, jotting his thoughts on paper back to his beginning, October 19, 1911. As the pages accumulated, he transcribed to a typewriter. Dad was really getting serious about this, so the family went out on a limb and purchased a computer! Statistics indicate that only 1 in 5 people over 70 use the computer. Dad was a bit intimidated at first. We compare our teaching him how to use the computer to him teaching us how to drive a "stick shift". Many fun times, aggravating times, times we wanted to give up, but in the end, we learned how to drive and dad entered the age of the computer. When he realized what it could do for him, he was very excited. Then he discovered the Internet…who says you couldn't learn to "surf" at 80! He became rapidly proficient. Dad enrolled himself in a correspondence course from the University of Virginia to improve his writing skills. What a life he's had. From horse and buggy to surfing' the net!

We are so proud of our father who now is 90 years old and has more energy than most around him. He works in the yard and has a beautiful garden. Volunteers his time with the Melbourne Police Department. For many years has been a leader for the AWANA kids club at his church. He still bakes every Saturday morning. He recently went airboat riding; white water rafting and still has time to write a book. What's next dad, skydiving?

Thank you Dad for taking the time to put your thoughts and memories to words. You have given us a rich heritage. You lead by example and challenge us and our future generations. You have given us one of life's greatest gifts, so much of yourself. The Book of Proverbs says it best" the just man walketh in his integrity: his children are blessed after him."

We love you Dad.

0-595-22737-6